Kermit — I know you already a lot of what's in here but I know you will find something good and use it.

Good Luck

Nick Fenger

usiness
est

The Manager as Coach

Remodel Your Management Style

by
T. Nick Fenger, Ph.D

D1557464

Encouragement Press

Information to Encourage Achievement

1261 West Glenlake
Chicago, IL 60660
www.encouragementpress.com

ISBN-13: 978-1-933766-31-7   ISBN-10: 1-933766-31-X

10 9 8 7 6 5 4 3 2 1

©2008 Encouragement Press, LLC
1261 W. Glenlake
Chicago, IL 60660
www.encouragementpress.com

Special discounts on bulk quantities of Encouragement Press books and products are available to corporations, professional associations and other organizations. For details, contact our Special Sales Department at 1.253.303.0033.

About the Author

T. Nick Fenger, Ph.D. has been a consultant and coach to Fortune 500 as well as smaller companies for over 25 years. Starting as an Organizational Psychologist and ultimately reaching the level of Executive Vice President of Human Resources of a successful venture capitol firm with roughly two dozen subsidiaries, he has developed training and coaching programs that have assisted hundreds of executive, middle managers and first line supervisors augment their ability to help their team members improve their technical and management skills. His writings and trainings have assisted those managers to coach and train their successors to advance in responsibility, some to be founders of their own companies.

Acknowledgement and Thank You

To the many people who have given their attention and encouragement to
risk being a coach; to my mother who coached me through my dyslexia; to
my father who coached me to find dropped screws (among other things)
in mountains of sawdust; to both who showed me how nature and people
work; to my son who turned lemonade stands into the means to make friends
and influence people; to my daughter who coaches teams which change the
world; and to my employers and readers who never stop asking questions to
challenge me contually to learn and write.

Table of Contents

Introduction

Chapter 1:
Preparing to Coach 5

Chapter 2:
What Coaching Is Not 11

Chapter 3:
What Coaching Is... 19

Chapter 4:
The Risks of Coaching... 37

Chapter 5:
Know to Whom You Are Talking.. 57

Chapter 6:
Coaching Approaches to Communication Issues 83

Chapter 7:
Coaching Approaches to Problem Solving Issues................. 105

Chapter 8:
Coaching Yourself 123

Chapter 9:
Coaching Your Boss... 131

Chapter 10:
How Well Do You Stack Up?.. 139

Chapter 11:
Perfect Practice Makes Perfect.. 147

Introduction

Why do sports teams have coaches? To win, of course! Players struggle to refine their shooting, hitting, throwing and scoring skills to develop their capabilities to beat the other teams. But their focus on their individual technical skills only occasionally allows them to develop the cooperation skills necessary to make a winning team. Working well together takes experience and a special understanding of the skills necessary to make the team successful. It is the job of the coach to help individuals work together to out score their opponents.

The same is true of business teams. Individuals may know how to invent, sell, plan or any of the many skills that are necessary for a company to win in their competition with other companies. It still takes someone to mold people together to come out ahead in the search to satisfy the customer.

Many players as well as employees are so good at what they do that they are tapped to take on the responsibilities of management and coaching. But it is well known that it is not always the best players or employees that make the best coaches. The task of coaching requires a special skill for helping people recognize that the job of winning requires cooperation and team work as well as top individual performance.

Cooperation requires communication and thinking ahead to know what to do when you have the ball. Employees need to know what to do when they pass on their work to the next person to make sure their efforts jell and their common goal is achieved. Everyone has the responsibility to make everyone else successful. Home run hitters and individual inventors have a role to play in business but the vast majority of scoring and achieving business results is accomplished by doing what the team needs when they need it.

In over 25 years of coaching both employees and neighborhood sports leagues, I have seen the similarities and differences between coaching both kinds of teams. The basic skills are different; the plays and plans are different; the people are different; and the customers are different. But how to coach for business success is very much the same as coaching sports. Coaching to achieve success is what this book is all about.

THE FOCUS OF THIS BOOK

This book explores how to add coaching skills to your present management style.

Professional business coaches have identified over 100 business functional areas where coaching has been employed. It is not the purpose of this book to discuss sales, production, executive issues or any other business function. Rather its purpose is to give you the skills you need to add coaching to your skill set. It is assumed the reader has a basic knowledge of the job functions in the areas in which you wish to coach your employees.

Business coaching seeks to understand the nature of work and how people respond to the demands of their job requirements. Coaching is management but management with a new set of special skills. This book presents those differences and discusses ways which will allow you to add those additional skills to how you manage.

After you have read about the fundamentals of coaching, you will be reminded of the famous words of Vince Lombardi: "Practice does not make perfect, perfect practice makes perfect." You will have the knowledge to examine what you do and how you can improve on what you do. Each chapter will have questions which should help you examine your progress and your learned skills to assist you in coaching for success. Formulating the answers to these questions will give you valuable insight about who you are and what you need to do to be a super bowl coach.

PricewaterhouseCoopers has been using coaching worldwide since 1998 and estimates returns average six times their investment. Manchester Consulting also showed a six times return. Part of that return comes in the form of internal efficiencies through fewer production and process errors, better quality work product and decreased turnover. The other part of that return comes in the form of competitive advantage through efficiencies in processing customer information and an improved ability to create new products and services.

This book is your first step in becoming a skilled business coach. Indeed, in order to more quickly perfect your coaching skills, you may wish to experience in person how a consulting coach goes about their work or even hire you own coach. But the information you gain from reading this book will give you a comprehensive picture of the foundations of business coaching and some techniques and methods you can use to incorporate those ideas into how you manage. The book shows you the amount of attention and work you should be prepared to expend in order to adopt and improve your management as a business coach. Finally, you will be introduced to the rewards you should expect when you practice new coaching behaviors.

T. Nick Fenger, Ph.D.

1

Preparing to Coach

Making a profit is the scoring system every company uses to determine wins and losses in the game of business. Having the right skills in the right job is the way a company wins decisively. Do you have the right skills in the right job? You may have been the person responsible for hiring the people who report to you. You may have had an opportunity to read their résumé and interview them or you may have found an unknown person sitting in a chair in your department who was hired by the human resource (HR) department. It does not make any difference how the person got her job or what you know about your employee, one thing you should understand as a coach: You will need to know them better.

You not only need to know their education and work background, you need to know how they work under pressure, how they use their time, how they go about communicating and solving problems. You will want to find out if they are comfortable and confident enough to admit they may have made a mistake and what new skills they need to learn. You need to know, too, whether they want to do their job better or just well enough to keep it.

Most managers have some sort of employment file that lists background and some information that has been obtained about the individual. Some companies keep that file in the HR department. You will likely forget many of the things you observe about an employee and much of what someone else tells you about a person. You need your own file and in it you should keep the answers to the questions you need to remember about how they use their time, and all the rest of the questions just discussed. Knowing the right information about an employee at the right time will be a very important part of your coaching efforts.

Build your coaching on the right information

MAKING YOUR LIST AND CHECKING IT TWICE

Make a list of the things you should learn about your employees, their values, limitations and special skills. Check off the things you have in the file so that when you look at that list you know at a glance what you have in your file and what you still need to find out.

You will never know everything about someone who reports to you but without this information it will be difficult for you to coach that person with understanding and efficiency.

In addition to knowing all you can about a person, you need to know all you can about the job they are doing. Most companies have a written job description. It is unlikely though that the description tells all that is necessary to be successful in that job. You and the team member will have to create the real picture of what should happen in that job.

Communication and problem solving are two competencies that you will need to find out about, because they are the basis of capable work. When the holder of the job must know how to communicate effectively with another person in the company, make a note of the name of that person and describe how well the two actually communicate. Also include any descriptions you have of how the person in the job solves the problems related to that job. Helping your employee improve his or her ability to talk with their co-workers to resolve problems will be critical moments when your coaching will make its biggest impact.

Few job descriptions even mention communications and problem solving but failures in these areas are the source of two-thirds of job terminations. Your task is to compare what you know about each employee with what that employee needs to accomplish to fulfill his job responsibilities. You may discover some holes in either his technical knowledge, knowledge of himself, your knowledge of him or what the demands of the job are. You may know something about an employee's skills but not know how she will apply them to her job. Or you may not know something about the responsibilities of a job and how she will address those demands. In any case learning more about the job-person match will be another source of the content of your coaching.

Now you know the basic models of coaching: 1) Assess the capabilities of the person and the requirements of the job they do; 2) determine what discrepancies exist between what the person does and what the job requires; then 3) encourage and assist them to improve. As you prepare to coach your employees, they and you must consider these differences. As you coach, you help them understand that success and job satisfaction come when we take our weakest skill and make it among our strongest. Those discrepancies become the issues that the coaching process attempts to adjust. You will look at those discrepancies often as you prepare yourself to coach and as you prepare your employees to be coached.

Help the worker see what their job needs

Many employees will not understand the motives and reasons why you are comparing a person and the requirements of a job description. They may be fearful or resentful until you help them understand that many employees struggle with some of the same issues; among them:

- Doing the job is more important than understanding how they do the job.
- Others do not understand their basic capabilities very well.
- Some believe they are capable of doing anything no matter what it is, including being the boss.
- Some are reluctant to admit that they have any limitations.
- Some have never attempted to be specific about what they can and cannot do.

- Others lack the experience of being challenged to try new things or to work harder or smarter, so are not familiar with what it takes to improve.

- Still others yet do not possess the capacity to believe that anyone else could ever correctly understand anything about them, including their manager.

So each type of employee will present special challenges to your coaching.

When every employee comes to expect that coaching centers around the four parts of the job/person analysis and how to make the match better, the fears and resentments should diminish. Once they realize you are there to help them achieve a higher level of personal success, fear and resentment should decrease even further.

After you have gone over the basics of the three part process, ask them to do their own assessment of themselves, their job, what discrepancies they see and their ideas about making changes. Encourage them to write it down. Write down your own impressions of the four parts of the job/person comparison for everyone you manage. These impressions will be your notes for later coaching sessions.

As you begin your discussions, do not try to jump into solving problems right away. Simply help them make the comparison of who they are and their job first. They will need to digest that information before they will know what kind of questions they and you will address. When you get together for your next discussion you will likely have some divergent views of the person, the job and the differences. But some of your observations will be similar, too. Make a list of the changes you see as possible. Discuss what and why they could be done. Find out what changes the employee would take responsibility for and how he would see himself approaching these changes. When he and you are prepared to tackle how to make those changes, both of you will be prepared to begin your coaching.

Assist the worker to do what the job needs

WHAT IS COACHING?

Coaching is the assisted self-evaluation of job performance and is focused on making improvements. Developing good coaching skills can be demanding and even risky. Reading this book will acquaint you with the basics you will need to become a coach. It will also walk you through several possible conversations you may have with your employees and help you incorporate changes in your management style and give you the knowledge you need to practice good coaching skills.

Questions to Ask Yourself

- What will it take for me to be a good coach for my employees?
- Do I know how to prepare my employees to engage in coaching?
- What do I need to learn about people in order to be a good coach?
- Do I know all I need to know about the jobs in my department to assist the people who hold those jobs to improve their abilities?
- What differences do I expect between the people who work for me and the jobs they are doing?
- Are the job descriptions in my department up-to-date?
- What should be done to revise the job descriptions of my department to be more accurate and helpful to me and my employees?
- Do I keep good notes on what my employees do in their jobs?
- What do I need to learn from this book about coaching to be prepared to do a good job as a coach?
- What is a definition of coaching?
- What does the word assisted mean in the definition?
- Is encouragement a part of coaching?
- Does a bigger salary encourage people to do a better job?
- How much of each job involves communications and problem solving?

- Do I recognize faulty communication and problem solving when I witness it?
- How do I correct those faults through coaching?
- Have I prepared myself to look for the answers to these questions in and outside of this book?

RESOURCES

For further reading, consider the following excellent books to help you improve your coaching skills:

An Introduction to Business Coaching, WorkGroup Resources, 1999

Coaching for Performance, Nicholas Brealey, 2002

2

What Coaching Is Not

Now that you know what it will take to add coaching to your management style, this chapter will help you to avoid obstacles that could make your coaching experience more difficult. You need to be aware that there are several myths many managers believe about coaching–and they are not accurate.

COACHING: *A Behind-the-Scenes, Hands-off Approach to Management*

Nothing could be further from the truth. Coaches are in the trenches and usually work harder than the average manager. They do not just watch. Sometimes they are even more involved in what their employees do because they have handed over a good deal of the responsibility to their employees to accomplish the required business results. It is true that the coach does not micromanage and does not attempt to know of all the little things that go on in her area of responsibility. But a management coach knows what each of her employees is responsible for and how each approaches his/her job.

In addition, a coach is aware of the basic fundamentals of how the business and technical processes work in the area of her group's efforts. She has a specific picture of how these processes work, and the communications and problem solving necessary for things to get done. She knows what her department must produce in order to contribute seamlessly to the efforts of all the departments in the company. She has a good feel for where each of her employees needs to grow in order to assume more responsibility as the company grows and as retirement and turnover open opportunities for advancement.

The coach must know these fundamentals better than her employees, otherwise she has little opportunity to help them effectively deal with the problems that come up and how to assist her employee fit the demands of his job. The coach is always testing herself about her knowledge of the fundamentals of each job in her business area. She is always asking herself what her employees need to know and what they really know. Individuals who report to the coach may have a better knowledge of the particular technical issues than the coach has. However, the coach is always helping those individuals find the areas in their knowledge that need to be improved. The coach asks people to keep her up-to-date on technical advancements, learning from them when possible. Her example of learning should be an encouragement to others for them to learn.

Is There a Set Formula for How a Manager Should Coach?

There are some fundamentals of good coaching but there is no formula for it. The demands of your coaching effort could change quickly. Business management has been conceived as a function where people plan, organize, direct and control; those functions are well understood and fairly standard in how they are done, according to Peter Drucker. The coach should be prepared to look at how all those functions need to be changed according to the business demands made upon the department. A coach may ask one of her employees to take responsibility for a project's planning and help him learn the planning process—or for that matter, any other task that may keep the department on track. Delegating authority and responsibility does not, however, remove the ultimate responsibility from the coach for helping the employee accomplish the job that has been delegated.

It is a fundamental principle of coaching that all employees should be treated fairly but that does not mean that all employees should be treated the same. Fairness in coaching means respecting the integrity of the individual. But respect means that how you help an employee to resolve the differences between what he does on the job and the needs of his job may require considerable creativity in your coaching. You must respect the individual's responsibility to perform his job in the manner that suits him because he is the one who fits his skills to the task. You are there primarily to help rather than do.

Coaching focuses on the person first then the job

Should People Who Make More Be Coached Differently?

As you compare the needs of the job and the skills of the person, money is not the primary consideration. How much you pay someone should not determine the manner in which you coach and the objectives of your coaching. You will not treat a million dollar a year employee with any more respect than someone who earns one twentieth that figure.

It is, after all, not the money that performs the job tasks. It is the person who performs them so it is the person that should be the focus of your attention. Different people will of necessity be coached on different things. You may ask a manager who has a larger budget to pay more attention to more details or more expensive items than the employee who has responsibility for a smaller budget. But you will ask the same questions and employ a similar coaching process with both of them as you attempt to help them learn and improve their capabilities.

Is the Performance Review the Proper Tool for Keeping Employees on Track?

As a coach your discussions with your employees will not be focused on how much their salaries are going to increase if they make changes in how they work nor how they compare with any of their fellow employees. Any mention of these issues will destroy your effectiveness as a coach. Your attention is on the person, the job and how well the person does the job as well as what improvements need to be made to how she handles the job. You may wish to change what the company pays an employee but discussing that issue with the employee comes after they have made the changes necessary to improve their performance. The idea that people work better when they are paid more or receive a big bonus is not a concept that works in coaching. Coaching helps the improvement happen before the bonus or raise is paid. Coaching focuses on improving how the job is done because the improvement needs to be made. Encouragement to do a better job can be a part of coaching but money is not a part of that encouragement. Most coaches let their HR department handle questions of remuneration. That way the issue of money does not cloud your coaching relationship.

Are Memos Good Coaching Tools?

The advent of e-mail and computer communication has been hailed by many managers as making their job easier because they can get ideas to their employees faster. You may wish to include the discussion of work changes in your e-mails but they are not coaching. Even if you are very specific about what kind of changes you wish your employee to make, your writing will likely require interpretation of what you are asking for. You will not really know if your employee has correctly understood your written directions and your employee will not really know if they have interpreted your directions correctly until you handle their questions in person. Many mistakes are made by an employee assuming that she adequately understands what you have tried to communicate in writing. Until she knows what you meant and you know she knows what you meant, you have not completed your coaching task.

Coaching Is Not Necessary when Senior Management Issues a Directive

Any attempt to justify to the employee that a requested change should be made because someone else suggested it, or that it is company procedure, or any reason outside of the employee's desire to make the change is not coaching. Such suggestions do not tap into the employee's own motivational sense of improvement. Ordering, demanding, micromanaging, manipulating, making false promises, withholding recognition or training, implying that you want agreeable yes-men to work for you, or requesting that someone try something new but not to rock the boat are neither viable management nor coaching techniques and will ultimately result in the employee backing away from risking a change.

When employees are faced with such manipulation they can rationalize that they do not understand what you are asking when they simply disagree with your methods. If you use such methods and make such statements, your employees will remain afraid to communicate their confusion or fears to you and will likely refuse to expend the effort to make the change you have requested. Any confusion or disagreement between themselves and your suggestions or demands will likely be stonewalled. And you may never discover why your employee somehow never made the change.

COACHES DO NOT GET ANGRY

We all know that this is not true. Some managers and coaches have made their reputations by expressing their anger vehemently. They believe that showing their anger gives the team players notice that the coach knows the right thing to do at any moment and the player better follow his instructions. Sometimes it works. But most managers who live by expressing their anger never find out, let alone, ask why the players respond the way they do. Some do try harder. Some respond by doing the opposite of what the coach has asked or even quit. Some actually make more mistakes because they panic.

Anger is a common response to frustration, difficulty and failure. Everyone can get angry. How the person deals with that anger is what differentiates a capable coach from a manager. The capable coach senses his anger and realizes his employees could be angry as well. The employees' anger is more important than the coach's anger because the employee is doing the job. The coach helps his employee evaluate how her anger might influence how she does the job. Some anger can motivate better performance. Some anger can create poorer performance, even avoidance. The coach controls his anger but uses it to recognize the possibility of the player's anger and helps the coach and the player find a focus for their anger that will improve the situation.

COACHING STIFLES CREATIVITY

On the contrary, coaching encourages creativity and the evaluation of the consequences of that creativity. Non-creative approaches to changing work processes are most likely not coached. Copying or borrowing solutions can be suggested and may be appropriate to the situation. But such suggestions usually occur only after an attempt to coach a creative change has failed and a more ready solution is called for.

INTIMIDATION CAN BE A NECESSARY TOOL TO MOTIVATE CHANGE

A good coach assumes any change that needs to be done can be done. A change may be a stretch for the employee but you and the employee need to understand that the challenge to change will be received and acted on in a positive fashion. Asking for the impossible is not coaching; it is a form of management insanity.

You need to know the employee well enough to understand that the change requested is something the employee can do, wants to do and will respond to by taking on the challenge. Impossible requests will create confusion at the least and intimidation and fear at the worst. But creating fear is not coaching. Coaching cannot effect change in an intimidating work atmosphere. Learning and risking new approaches to a task occur when the employee believes she can take on a new challenge to make something new happen and understand that mistakes will be evaluated not punished. Learning and risking do not happen when the possibility of intimidation or harsh criticism exists.

Coaching does not work in an atmosphere of threat

COACHING IS NOTHING BUT DISGUISED COUNSELING

It is true that coaches, counselors and therapists have special relationships with the people with whom they work. But each role is different. A therapeutic relationship assumes there is some severe mental illness or deeply hidden problem that has to be diagnosed and treated. An individual consults with a counselor because he is aware that a specific personality problem or disorder exists which blocks or limits the individual from establishing or achieving life goals such as basic schooling, establishing effective family relationships or attaining work skills. These problems and disorders may cause people to engage in dysfunctional and self defeating relationships or lead them to disobey laws or harm other people through carelessness or selfishness.

Coaching, on the other hand, is a relationship that assumes the individual has developed adequate work skills and can function effectively as a team member or be in a position that demands individual control and effective communication. This includes the ability to focus on short- and long-term business goals and objectives. Coaching does not pretend to deal with mental illness or personality defects. Those problems may exist in the work place but employee assistance programs have been incorporated into the modern business environment to deal with the presence and severity of those issues. Coaching limits itself to focus on such issues as poor communications, ineffective problem solving, lack of cooperation in team work and the development of employees to increase their professional skills and to assume more work responsibility. A coach does not presume to be capable of taking on personality dysfunction or mental instability.

Questions to Ask Yourself

- Do I understand that motivation for change comes from the employee rather than from their manager or coach?
- What are ways that I can communicate support to the employee so he will be motivated to make a change?
- In what ways might I inadvertently limit the effort that an employee will put into making a change on the job?
- If I tell an employee exactly what he must do on the job does that mean I am not coaching?

- How do I respond when my employees bring me work changes that they thought of themselves?
- Do I communicate an it-is-not-any-good-unless-I-suggest-it attitude?
- Am I interested in maintaining control over what happens in my department rather than encouraging innovation?
- Do my employees find my ideas helpful or do they pursue them only because I am the boss?
- How do I really know what an employee thinks of any idea I may suggest?
- Do I encourage sharing of ideas between employees?
- Do I encourage my employees to keep secrets from other departments?
- Do I show people that I value a good idea?

- If I work in a company that prefers tried and true ways, how can I encourage my employees to innovate?
- What has to change in a conservative company to allow new ideas to be implemented?
- Which management styles do not fit with the practice of good coaching?
- What kinds of employee issues does a coach deal with and which kinds does he refer to other company or health professionals?
- What other questions do I need to ask myself?

RESOURCES:

This is a highly-recommended classic book which will supplement the concepts learned:

Stop Managing, Start Coaching, Irwin, 1996

3

What Coaching Is

Everyone is different. Employees may have the same production objectives and do the same job but they do it differently. The company may have a certain process installed for the team but each employee uses a common process in their own particular way. Employees do things differently because they are different people. They will respond to your coaching differently, too. Coaching is not a one-size-fits-all process. You must build an individualized picture of each of your employees and you should be prepared to coach different people differently.

What does a different picture of each of your employees get you? It gets you out of the rut of trying to get everyone to do things in the way you think they should be done. It allows you to see people as themselves instead of as interchangeable parts of the wheels that turn and mesh in the company. Individual pictures of individual people allow you to be free and more objective in your perspective about how the same job could be done differently.

Jobs with the same name are not the same job if different people do them. Different pictures of similar jobs allow you to concentrate on helping the individual tackle the job instead of thinking that the job is more important than the individual. Concentrating on the individual allows you to look at the individual as the most important part of the job-person connection. It allows you to change the job to fit the individual if necessary instead of always thinking that the individual must be fit to the job.

Coaching focuses on the individual

When you focus on individual differences, everyone wins, you, the employee and the company. Having a different picture of each of your employees allows you to see the person improve the job rather than the job determining what the individual does. It allows you to see an individual growing in skills and satisfaction and learning to do other jobs. It allows you to consider if the individual could assume your job someday and what you must do to prepare that person for your job.

Having a different picture of each of your employees implies that you, too, must look at yourself in a more effective way. Instead of only trying to fit yourself to your job it allows you to be sensitive to the issues you like and dislike about what you do. It allows you to see yourself more objectively and so see your employees more effectively. It allows you to imagine what you might do to improve yourself and so better understand how other individuals might improve themselves. It allows you to experience how you have grown and what choices you made in order to develop the capabilities that you mastered in order to assume your present position. Seeing your employees as individuals expands your perspective of the value of individuals and allows you to coach yourself to change and help you to be open to how your boss can coach you to change.

Seeing your employees as individuals puts a whole different perspective on your job, your place in your company, the individuals who report to you, their capabilities and responsibilities. It is this different perspective that will help you be more creative and do a better job of coaching and managing. It makes your job more complicated but easier at the same time. Instead of just getting your job finished, you can concentrate on how to work with each of your employees to make them (and you) more successful.

Coaching will change you from a person who must have all the answers into a leader who allows others to learn and have some answers. Many managers have been amazed at the excellent solutions proposed for vexing problems when coached in an atmosphere of encouragement and trust. When you know others have answers too, you can build a team whose members are capable of stepping in at any minute to give others a hand. Coaching helps people not only get work done but get it done more effectively and efficiently. And as you gain the respect of your employees, they will help you do your job so you can learn more and so be able to move on to more and bigger responsibilities. Learning to be a coach is worth it.

How Is Coaching Accomplished?

The simple answer: not through giving directions but by asking questions. Questions help you get information as well as present issues to others in a way that helps your employees think about what they need to examine in order to grow on the job. A well-phrased question begs for information; but as the employee looks for the answer they have to test themselves about what they really know about the subject of the question. Answering a question may stretch their knowledge. When they stretch their knowledge they frequently find they need to do even more thinking by challenging themselves to create a better response.

Coaching facilitates thinking and making changes. Questions help employees think through how they will make those changes happen. Questioning helps open the employees' minds as they examine what they do and what leads them into areas they may not have examined before.

Examples of Questions to Ask in Creating an Environment in Which Change Happens with Acceptance

- Have you found any means of doing things more quickly or more adequately since you took over this job?
- What challenges have you faced and how have you overcome them?
- Would you do anything differently?
- Have you asked for help from someone who has more experience in doing the job?
- Have they been helpful to you?
- Have you met your goals?
- What has been the toughest item you have had to do in order to make progress here?

> - Is there anything that tests your capabilities and patience on your job?
> - Do you like to be challenged?

COACH RESPONSIBILITY

As discussed previously, telling an employee how to do something is usually not an effective way to coach. Yes, giving the answer to the problem may get something done quickly, but may not achieve the lasting effects coaching can produce. The problem with giving orders is that something may be done automatically but without understanding the reasons for the action. And it may be what your employee thinks you want regardless of what the situation actually demands–the very thing that should not be done.

Why is coaching superior to telling? To please the boss, is an unwritten rule for most employees. After all, how many times have you heard from a manager during your orientation to work: Please make sure you do what you think is right rather than what you might think I might want done in a situation. I will always respect your ability and insist that you follow your own well-thought intentions in preference to mine as you resolve a problem. Probably never.

No wonder then, that when an employee responds to her boss' request, her response is usually to do it the boss' way even if she secretly disagrees with it. But, if you, the boss, tell your people what you want done, do your employees really know how you specifically want it done? Probably not, unless you specify every action you think should occur and under every possible condition or event. Even then what you want may not be the way your request is followed. Will your employee add some of their own style or timing to your answer to the problem? Very likely. If you have to spend a great deal of time clarifying what you want after your employee adds a little of their own creativity, how much time have you saved by insisting they do it your way? None. Now look at what else you have sacrificed by wanting it done your way: You have lost an opportunity to facilitate their learning how to attack the problem from a point of view that is new to them but which they own and which may be superior to your own solution.

Coaching questions focus on responsibility

Of course, if you are known to give good directions, some employees will have learned how you like tasks done and will try their best to do it your way. But the question still remains: Is doing it your way always the best way? Maybe your employee knows some thing about the problem you do not. After all, he is the one who is right in the middle of it. It is possible things have changed since you saw the situation the last time? So who is better prepared to attack the problem: You with the experience of having faced and solved that kind of problem a while ago, or the employee who is on the spot? Maybe neither. Maybe the best solution to the problem will come out of a collaboration between you and the employee. And if your collaboration (yes, coaching is collaboration) works out well, you will have given your employee and yourself an opportunity to learn something new.

So, if you do not spell out each step of the way, what is the way to set up a coaching relationship that will work effectively? The good coach sets up a process where the employee retains the responsibility for resolving the situation while the coach assumes the responsibility of questioning the employee through the problem stage to an appropriate solution. The coach starts where the employee is, trying to understand the problem from the employee's point of view, and then creates a solution that the employee owns.

The coach does not ask questions in order for the coach to show he knows the answer. He asks questions that the employee needs to ask which will allow her to state the problem, look for, and find an answer. The coach wants the employee to learn by leading the employee to follow his questions as well as pose her own questions. Facilitating employees to ask their own questions is critical to the employees taking ownership of the responsibility for resolving the issue and to their development of new and better skills in question asking. A good coach facilitates the development of good questioning in the employees so the coach does not always have to be there to ask the questions. A good coach encourages his employees to develop their own questions. The difference between just being a coach and being a good coach is the difference between asking questions mainly for information and asking questions that help your people learn to think for themselves.

Appropriate Questions to Ask to Help Your Employee Realize and Accept Their Responsibilities

- What do you think the problem is?
- Do you think you have a sufficient handle on the nature of the problem to proceed to resolving it?
- Do you think you know more about this problem than I do? (When they say yes your response is always good!)
- Is there something specific about this situation you do not understand?
- Who is really responsible here, you or me? (If they balk, ask: Are you the one who is in the middle of the situation and has to get it resolved?)
- How can I give you some help without doing your work?
- If I were not here where could you get some insight into the situation?
- Do you feel capable of dealing with the issue (without my help, on your own)?
- Do you now feel capable of coaching someone else how to handle this issue?

Coaching Facilitates Learning

Learning means being able to repeat it more than once in the appropriate circumstances. How many times has someone said: Sure that makes sense, I will change that, then proceeded to fail to make the new behavior a permanent difference in how they do their job? One time does not a habit make. Maybe they are agreeing with you just to get you off their back. In any case, a prudent coach circles back to ensure that the change is performed on a regular basis. Repetition confirms learning.

As the coach you must know an efficient way to perform whatever it is you are coaching. In certain supervisory situations you may not know how to perform a complicated technical process or procedure. So in place of knowing how to do it, you need to know where to find a description of what that action or procedure should be. Failing either to know what the process is, or how to find a description of the process to facilitate its learning, takes you out of the coaching role and puts someone else in it. Thus the coaching may come from a teacher, professor or colleague. You will depend upon their insight and understanding (in addition to the employee's) to determine what your employee could and should be learning to do.

One thing to avoid here is assuming that you have to tell your employee everything about how to proceed. Finding out how to do something by himself can often produce a better learning process for the employee. Finding out by himself will help the learning become permanent. Indeed, telling an employee what to do and how (even if you present a cogent rationale) may interfere with his desire to do it at all, let alone regularly. Not-invented-here can be a significant put off for many employees so be open to consider using solutions the employee suggests. And do not expect that the change will become a habit over night. Most people learn to improve the fit of a habit to their own comfort level by repeating something over time and in different contexts.

Coaching Emphasizes Learning: Questions to Ask
- Is the change working for you?
- How difficult a process was it to do XYZ on a regular basis?
- Has it become second nature now that you have had time to practice ABC?
- Are you getting better results now that you are performing the new procedure?
- What did you have to change to get it right?
- What changes have occurred since you started the new procedure?
- Has anyone else noticed how much better you are doing XYZ?
- What kind of savings in time (or money, or rejects) has your new process realized?
- Are there more things to do (change) to get it right (comfortable) on a regular basis?
- What other questions can you invent to check to see that the learning is well established?

Coaching Means Seeing Things Differently but Not too Differently

Most of us would not be able to comb our hair, adjust our tie or scarf, or improve our golf swing or tennis backhand without getting a different perspective on what we are doing. Sometimes we use a mirror, sometimes a video replay, or sometimes a coach to give us hints or feedback as to what we are doing that we might change.

A coach in business does much the same thing as a mirror or video. He sees what we are doing that needs to change and he asks us to take a look at a possible change, sometimes through a mental picture, sometimes through a verbal hint.

A significant point to be aware of in coaching is that the hint cannot be too radical a departure from what was being done before. Too much information can be no information when what has to be changed is too complex for the employee to put into action. That is one reason why the boss' do-it-this-way suggestion may not be a good idea, especially when it is too different from what the employee is doing already. The key to good coaching is focusing on one small task at a time and in a way that the employee has a better chance to see what is wrong and know what to do to make the change. Too much information can cause confusion and frustration.

Coaching, to be successful, must elicit or provide insights that help connect ideas which were previously too far apart to see their connection. Sometimes the individual makes the connection himself, sometimes the coach helps make the connection for him, but in the end the person being coached must appreciate the new connection, otherwise the employee is still in the dark and the coaching process has failed.

Questions for Good Coaching
- Can the action steps be broken down further to make them easier?
- How does A relate to B?
- What has to happen in order to get from Y to Z?
- Is it automatic or does someone (some process) have to help it happen?
- What happens if Z is not reached?

- Does anything have to be invented to accomplish X?
- Have you drawn a picture (diagram) to make the relationship clear?
- Can anyone understand it or will training have to occur to get it in place?
- What is different about what you propose?
- Is your idea too good (complex) to be learned easily?

COACHING ENABLES CHANGE

Change comes from the employee accepting the need for change. Perhaps the employee will bring a need for improvement to you but not understand why this is happening. Or he may deny he has any need to do something differently at all. So not only do you have to look carefully at the employee to understand what he needs to do to change, but he has to look at himself to understand the need to change. If he does not accept the need for change, your suggestions or even orders to change, will likely not get very far.

Once you have established in your mind an individual's need for change, you have to encourage and establish their acceptance of that fact: Do you see (understand) improvement is necessary? (If the response is silence, ask: What could happen if nothing different is done? If the answer is: Nothing really needs to be done, you need to ask: Why do you think that?) What do you think needs to be done differently? Do you believe you can do it differently (better)? Do you accept (recognize) that you need to do XYZ? Will you change how you do ABC? How can I (someone else) help you deal with XYZ? Should I write that down for you? Should we go over (do) that together? How will you know you are doing it differently (correctly)? All are good questions that will help your employee specify the necessary change and accept the responsibility for making it. Some call that buying in.

Change requires learning; Learning demands change

COACHING IS COMMUNICATION

Communication can only take place when respect is shown. Would other managers listen to you if you cut them off or showed disdain for their comments? If they thought you should be ignored might not your employees think so too? If you want to be listened to and be respected yourself, show respect to others. Demonstrating interest shows respect. Allowing the employee time to respond to your questions shows respect. Encouraging learning shows respect. Helping the employee be responsible for making changes in his job shows respect.

Without respect coaching and even communication cannot occur. Every communication says I need something or I think you need something. Without respect, understanding what anyone needs is problematical. What a coach needs is the knowledge that her employees are actively working on the improvements that need to be implemented in their jobs. What an employee needs is the knowledge that his coach accepts the responsibility that her employee needs her questions and insight into his job situation.

COACHING IS ONE-ON-ONE BUT HAS VALUE FOR TEAMS

Communication between coach and employee has to happen on a regular basis in order to maintain the respect and trust that makes coaching effective. In organizations where coaching is not practiced, employees often complain that they see the organization as sterile. Working in their cubicles creates loneliness rather than giving the employees an experience of cooperation and group support. Research by Manchester Consulting has shown that in organizations where coaching is not practiced, it is much more difficult to create interdepartmental teams to facilitate work coordination and the gathering of diverse skills to achieve high productivity on complicated projects.

In organizations where coaching is practiced, employees have a much better understanding of the various skills and value of diversely assigned employees. And research by several Fortune 500 companies has shown that employees who have received coaching have improved levels of communicating with co-workers about a broader range of subjects and problems and so are much more productive than employees who have not received one-on-one coaching.

COACHING INCREASES FEEDBACK

The usual manager gives a performance review once a year. The performance review was invented because most managers do not give much feedback to their employees so it became important to insure that information was shared at least periodically. Coaches who engage employees once then disappear accomplish little. Coaching requires work habits to be examined on a more frequent basis. Coaching asks employees to assess their own behavior. If the employee is accurate in her assessment, the coach can confirm his perceptions. If the employee is not accurate the coach can ask the team member to reconsider certain situations and he can help the employee see them in a different perspective.

The increased number of contacts between the coach and the employee allows the coach to give more feedback to the individual. And as coaching improves communication between team members, it also allows more feedback among co-workers to improve their ability to work effectively together. Employees who have received individual coaching and work in teams have cited improved feedback from team members as being responsible for improved team success.

Questions to Ask

- How are things going?
- Are you getting well acquainted with how to make things happen?
- Can I answer any questions you might have?
- Do you think your co-workers are cooperative and helpful?
- How do you respond when others ask for your help?
- Do you thank people when they help you out?
- Did I thank you when you went out of your way to do what I asked?
- May I point out something I think you should be aware of?
- How would you evaluate your performance in the last week or so with your team?
- Any, No, or could be better, response to these questions gets a: Tell me what you mean, request.

Sometimes a question can be a more powerful way of giving corrective feedback because it asks the employee to remember that the coach did, indeed, give his feedback. Also, asking permission to give negative feedback in a positive way can make it easier for the employee to deal with criticism rather than just reject it because he feels afraid or hurt.

It is important that the coach ask for the employee to look at himself critically before she gives her observations. Often the employee will already have recognized that some improvement is needed. Then the coach can give positive feedback that the employee is paying attention to their performance. In this way a potentially negative situation becomes a positive one. If the employee is not aware of the needed change, the coach has opened the issue that a change is necessary in a constructive rather than a negative or critical way.

Questions to Encourage Change
- How have things been going recently?
- What has gone well?
- Is there anything you might want to improve?
- Have you sought critical help from anyone?
- May I make a suggestion?
- Have I been able to offer you some good advice in the past?
- Are you ready to deal with some suggestions now?

COACHING FACILITATES PROBLEM SOLVING

Most managers would perceive this subject as a given: Of course coaching solves problems, if it does not why do it? No one can count the variety of problems that need to be addressed in every business, some more complicated than others. Most of us think we know how to approach the problems we are familiar with. But what about those that we are unfamiliar with? Coaching can be helpful with both the familiar and the unfamiliar.

When something does not work it is usually a broken part (process) that needs fixing. So we try to find that broken something. In complicated situations there may be a series of connected broken somethings that need fixing. Coaching can help us avoid running off with the first idea that comes to mind believing that what was broken last time must be what is broken now and that the old solution is the best.

Your job as a coach is to help your employee develop the patience to do a thorough process of analyzing the symptoms to help pin point the cause; otherwise a lot of time could be wasted fixing things that are not broken. A coach slows down the doing to incorporate consideration of all aspects of the problem; the doing then is careful, multifaceted and well thought out. The chapter on problem solving will present several examples to help you master the skill of helping your employees be more thoughtful before they charge on to doing.

Some ways to encourage your employees to look beyond the obvious include helping them find out when the break occurred. Tying down the time and the other events that may have happened concurrently with the breakdown is one of the most important considerations to help find the cause(s). Knowing when and under what circumstances the part or process worked is also important. Another difficulty in problem solving that a coach can assist with includes: not describing the problem specifically enough to know exactly what is or is not involved in the problem. Without coaching, some of us forget that the size of the problem (i.e., ounces or tons) is also important to take into consideration.

Most of our problem solving efforts create an action plan after we find a cause. That is, who does what and when to deal with the cause. But many people are anxious to get on with matters and forget to do an analysis of what could go wrong with that plan. A good coach checks to see if there are any possible negative consequences of their employees' actions. Potential negative impacts that will likely happen need to be specified and an antidote planned for. Most business action plans really need a good plan B to be ready in case plan A falters or is flawed.

Besides finding cause for mechanical problems, how can one find a cause for problems that involve people? People problems arise because somebody wants something: Maybe they just plain want it (keeping up with the Joneses) or lament they cannot have it (because of scarce resources) or they are afraid of it (avoiding failure or other unpleasantness)—whatever it may mean to each individual.

People problems can usually be understood by determining a person's motivation. By finding out and supplying what they want (answering needs), people problems can often be resolved. Finding the motive is an important part of solving a murder case. Finding the motive can be difficult in people, but having insight into why people do things is important for a coach to uncover in resolving people issues. Knowing why you want something is one of the keys to understand how you interact with others in your characteristic manner. Often a coach can help us reflect upon ourselves and our own motives to facilitate better co-worker cooperation.

Coaching Questions to Facilitate Better Problem Solving
- What, when, where, and who are involved in the problem?
- What must a solution do to meet all the goals you want to achieve?
- What are the alternatives you have not chosen to pursue?
- Who will do what and when to resolve it?
- How much will it cost?
- How do you know?
- Have you tried anything that has not worked and why did it not?
- Have you thought of what might go wrong with your plan?
- What is the probability and impact of X happening?
- What will be your response when that happens?
- How do you know your response will be effective?
- What do they want?
- What else might satisfy them?
- How do you know?
- If you do nothing, what possible consequences are there?
- Are you prepared to stake your reputation on what you are about to do? Why (not)?
- Will it help to understand your motivation if we talk about it?

COACHING DEMANDS EXECUTION

All the questions, discussion, suggestions and thought in the world are worthless until some real change is made. Progress happens when actions take place that did not happen before. Many people do not do something unless they see someone else do it successfully (learning by example); while for others, action becomes possible when the situation has been thought through to the point of believing success might be possible. When understanding is present, effective action becomes possible. But something else needs to be in place: an absence of a fear of failure. Fear of failure is the most common cause of inaction. The task of coaching is to help the employee develop the confidence that he can handle any complication so solutions can get under way. The job of the coach is to help the employee understand and accept that the possible is almost inevitable because every bug is understood and every contingency can be handled.

Fear of failure takes different forms and seldom does a person understand that the reason they are not accomplishing something is because of this fear. Fear hides behind a number of activities that people substitute for working: Bragging to others about success; insisting that other people fix the problem (rather than working themselves to achieve success); citing fatigue or disinterest; excessive absenteeism; making excessive demands of others while excusing yourself; and making an excuse that others do not respect you; believing optimism and encouragement are the only elements of success; insisting on a certain work environment; excusing inactivity and a host of other excuses all try to hide fear and a lack of motivation. Replacing the excuse with focused work is the way coaching deals with these issues.

Coaching gets it done right

Follow-up Questions
- Have you looked at everything?
- What is the worst that can happen?
- Can you handle that?
- Is everything in place and everyone ready?
- If delay X arises, how will you handle it?
- How does this activity achieve real results?
- Do you feel anxious (confident)?
- What has happened to stand in your way of getting things underway?
- What are you considering when you feel anxious?

> • What has to happen for your anxiety to be resolved?
> • When do things get started?
> • Why then if not now?
> • Do you really want to get on with it?

COACHING FOSTERS EXCELLENCE AND SUCCESS

Making a change that becomes a habit and gets good results for which the employee gets recognized and rewarded is one giant step on the path to success. Following what the coach suggests brings some success for the coach, because he said it and he helped someone else get it done. But when the coach encourages an employee to pursue an idea that they have both examined and that idea is successful, should it not be the employee who reaps the success because she did it? It does not make any difference that her coach asked the questions. She found the answers and she now knows what questions to ask herself when she meets another situation like this one.

Feedback and questions about what a person can change are very powerful tools to start the change process. Positive feedback announces success. Success breeds success. When an employee learns to ask herself good questions, she can ask good questions of others. There is no end to the number of successful people coaching can influence.

Yesterday, the employee you coached through the problem solving process came to you with a suggestion to make a change that could add to your company's bottom line. She had worked out the specifics of why the situation exists, and an action plan to install it, (she presented a full analysis of all the possible alternatives and explained why the one she wants to do should be the most efficient and effective one). She also specified the potential problems that might get in the way of completing the project successfully and what could be done about them. She has learned to ask herself the questions you coached her to ask. Is now the right time to share your encouragement?

Here are the questions to ask yourself:

• Do I understand the reasons for asking questions rather than giving answers?

• How have I employed asking questions in the past?

- Do I give positive feedback when people give good answers and think?
- Do I understand the process of working through a problem with an employee?
- Do I believe there is a solution to every problem?
- Do I believe that there is no failure, only feedback for a better solution?
- What do I need to learn in order to be a better coach?
- What do I need to practice in order to be an effective coach?
- Do I have someone who is ready to do my job effectively?
- If I do not have someone, what are the skills that I need to look for?
- If I find a good candidate what do I need to do to prepare them effectively?
- What are all the steps that go into achieving results?
- Do I know how to assist people in order to help them become achievers?
- What might stand in the way of an individual being successful?
- What questions do I need to ask in order to help a person be successful?
- What is the single most important thing that coaching needs to achieve?
- Might a person define success in different terms than I would?
- Might a person define success in different terms than my company would?
- How can I recognize those differences in people and help them apply their perspectives to their job?
- Does everyone enjoy learning? Why not?
- How do I foster an appreciation for learning through coaching?
- How do I know a person wants to assume responsibility for achieving results?
- If I ask a person to make a change how do I know they will be willing to try to accomplish it?
- Can I predict how people will respond to my questions?
- Do people respond to risk in different ways? Why?

- How do I help a person to see a change as beneficial and want to make it?

- How do I help a person assess risk in making a change?

- Is coaching what I thought it would be?

- How does the description of coaching in this book fit with my perception of what I need to do to be a coaching manager?

- How comfortable am I with what I have learned up to this point?

- What do I need to learn from the rest of this book about coaching?

RESOURCES

Even experienced coaches need additional resources and training; consider the following:

Coaching for Peak Employee Performance, Richard Chang Assoc., 1997

Teaching Smart People How to Learn, Harvard Business Review, 1991, May/June.

4

The Risks
of Coaching

When you started to read this book you had an idea you might want to be a manager that used a coaching style. So far coaching has been described as:

- A style of management that explores rather than coerces;
- focuses on the employee;
- uses questions;
- encourages change and learning to improve how things are done; and
- focuses on results.

It would be nice if adopting a coaching style of management guaranteed better business results. But insurance companies have not yet brought out a product that insures against being a poor manager or being an ineffective coach. Here are some risks you should be aware of as you seek to coach:

- Making a change in your management style may create an opportunity for failure.
- What happens if your company does not want you to change?
- What happens when you ask the wrong question?
- How do you work through unfamiliar territory?
- What happens when an employee tries a change that fails?

- Where do you find the extra time to coach?
- Just asking an employee to change can create debilitating fear.
- How do you coach when you think someone is making up excuses and does not want to put out any effort to create change?
- Coaching may create competition among your employees.
- Coaching can create conflict.

MAKING A CHANGE IN YOUR MANAGEMENT STYLE HAS ITS RISKS

Why did you pick up this book? Was it because you heard about coaching and are just curious about what it is or are you aware that your management style needs to be improved? You can make some small improvements in your management by adopting some of the simpler aspects of coaching. One good element of coaching to adopt would be to incorporate asking more questions of your employees. Good questions always get more information and get people thinking about what they do and why.

Another good coaching element to adopt is an understanding that focusing on learning is a valuable approach to improving the productivity of your people. In fact, many companies insist that employees take seminars to improve their skills. You could likely add both approaches of questioning and active learning to your management style and help some important improvements occur.

But what happens if your boss or employee does not want you to change your management style or does not like it after you have made the change?

Many executives have risen to the top of organizations giving strong directions and closely controlling how everything is done. They may see their direct style as saving time and allowing them to closely monitor every aspect of what happens in their department. And they may have difficulty allowing you to adopt a more employee-centered style because allowing individual employees to do things differently may feel chaotic if not completely out of control. Maintaining conformity is often an unwritten but very strong rule in some businesses and the demand for conformity may dictate the style of your management.

Coaching does not generate automatic applause

Some employees, too, expect a very orderly and consistent work atmosphere. They might feel uncomfortable and complain if more responsibility is passed on to them, especially if they are new to some tasks or have difficulty assuming responsibility for others already. As you assess the possibility of introducing a coaching style of management, you will need to determine how your boss and employees would respond to your new emphasis on questioning, change and learning. Any reluctance on their part should be a warning. Little changes can grow into big issues especially when unexpected or first encountered. Those big issues could mean trouble for how people see you as a manager and might create animosity that would interfere with achieving the improvement in results you and the company seek. Follow the conversation between a team member and his manager

Coach: Have you ever worked with a manager who used a coaching style before?

Employee: I do not think so, what is that?

C: What kind of a relationship do you think you might have with a coach?

E: Someone who stands on the sidelines and tells me how to do things?

C: What does standing on the sidelines mean?

E: Not doing it for me, watching me work.

C: What kind of things might he talk to you about?

E: Reminding me about my mistakes, encouraging me to try new things, showing me what I could do differently.

C: Would you welcome this kind of help from me?

E: That is your job, is it not?

C: Yes, but I am wondering if we can develop a way of working together that helps you look at what you do and I might ask you to do some things that may be confusing and appear difficult.

E: I hardly think I would like that. But you are supposed to tell me how to do them so I do not make mistakes, are you not?

C: I may not do that all the time. There will be some occasions when I will ask you to try something without me telling you how.

E: Well, I am not used to that for sure.

C: How do you think you would respond to the responsibility of trying something new then going over it with me to learn and finding the confidence to tackle new things?

E: I do not know.

C: Probably not right now. If you feel uneasy about what I have asked you, would you be honest and tell me so? That way we can talk about it more before you do it?

E: I guess so, just as long as you promise me you are not going to stick me out on some limb all by myself.

C: I will try to help you by figuring out what kind of limb you are on and making it feel as strong as you need it to go further. Will that help?

E: Maybe could.

C: Do you think you will be able to learn that way?

E: Maybe.

C: Will you welcome an opportunity to learn from trying something?

E: Guess so.

C: Then we will both see about that, right?

E: Sure will.

This conversation appears to have helped your employee come to some acceptance of your efforts to include coaching in your approach to managing. It is a start in the process.

What Happens If You Ask the Wrong Question?

This is a good issue to explore before you begin your questioning process. There are some questions you want to avoid. The do-not-ask questions include those which pry into personal lives, carry subtle criticism or questions that beg a particular answer especially an answer that you want to hear. (Why did you not consider my idea?) Questions which do not get to the heart of the matter at hand usually only waste time. A question which deals with the specific issue at hand is the preferable question to ask. But some people have difficulty with direct questions. With them, going at the same issue from several different perspectives may be a more effective approach. Here is a conversation to avoid:

C: I see you are down on your production this month. Why?

E: The special materials I asked for did not arrive. I could do nothing about it.

C: Are you sure? When things do not arrive as you expect them, it is your responsibility to find out why and fix the problem if you can. Right?

E: I did ask about them but I could not get a straight answer out of the order department or the warehouse.

C: When you did not get any answers why did you not come to me?

E: Well, you have been asking me to take more initiative about resolving problems so I asked them to follow up. I did not want you to believe that I was not trying to take responsibility.

C: Well, how far did you think you could take responsibility before you had to get my authority to move the situation along?

E: As long as they acted like they were doing something to find out and get the problems worked out I thought I was doing what you thought I should.

C: But did you see any real improvement in what was happening?

E: No.

C: OK. So why did you not come to me?

E: I just did not think that was what you wanted me to do.

C: Well, how are you going to know that if you do not talk to me?

E: Good question. I will do that all the time now.

C: But only if you need to.

E: OK, when is that?

C: Do you not know by now?

E: Guess not.

What is wrong about the questions this coach asks? In this conversation, notice the criticism that he manages to sneak through to the employee. So much so in fact that not upsetting the manager appears to be as much or more of a concern than the actual reduction in productivity. It looks like this conversation can go round and round and where it will stop no one knows. Avoiding inappropriate criticism is an important part of coaching.

Questions which carry a critical tone should not be asked. Also, note what the employee learned in this conversation: Responsibility is expected but the responsibility he should take is to ask the coach. Is that a good or poor lesson in encouraging responsibility? Here is a preferable conversation:

C: Have you been keeping track of your production this month?

E: I am sure you have, otherwise you would not be asking me this question.

C: You are partially right. I have a feeling production is off, but I do not have any real figures. I am not trying to rub your nose in bad news but curious if you have some data on your production?

E: Yea, I know I am down, and I know exactly, by 16. Does that answer your question?

C: It does. I am glad to know you have been keeping track of it. What has been happening?

E: The special materials I ordered did not arrive when they were supposed to.

C: Did you get some good explanations as to the reason?

E: No.

C: How did you respond when your questions did not get good answers?

E: I thought about coming to you but asked if they could find out what the problem was and tried to find out if it was going to happen regularly.

C: That still meant you were not going to be able to keep up your production did it not?

E: Yes, but I had enough materials to do some subassemblies so I could catch up when the special materials came in finally.

C: Well, at least you were trying to use your time to get things done. But did you understand that working on subassemblies while not making the complete parts would not meet our supply commitments?

E: I did not think of that. I just thought using my time and catching up later would be what you wanted me to do. I was trying to take responsibility like you have been asking me to do.

C: Certainly the way you have done it is one way to use your time well. Did you ask anyone, though, when production was short this month if you had the authority to make the decision you did?

E: No.

C: OK. So we now have a couple issues to think through: What to do when special materials do not get here in a timely manner and if making more subassemblies then making up the short number of finished assemblies is a change you can make on your own. Right?

E: Right.

C: Well the lack of availability of special materials was the initial problem so we will tackle that one first. OK?

E: Yea.

C: What else could you have done beside make subassemblies?

E: No idea.

C: Is there anyone you could have consulted with who might have given you some ideas?

E: Yea, the boss of the warehouse. He could have gotten some better answers for me. You could have talked to him too. I could have asked shipping if they needed the whole assembly before I could finish the subassemblies and get the special materials delivered.

C: All good ideas. We do not know which would be the best now but do you see that just doing anything may not be the kind of responsibility you need to take?

E: Yea.

C: So rather than just making a decision that allows you to do something you think you can do, it would be helpful to find out what kind of a decision will make the best alternative for our company and our customers, right?

E: Makes sense.

C: What would you do differently now?

E: Get someone to put pressure on supply and check if making subassemblies would meet our commitments.

> C: So taking responsibility does not always mean doing something; it means doing the things that will get our objectives met, right?
>
> E: Right.

This conversation takes twice as long as the first one. But the coach has skillfully led the employee to consider different actions and their consequences. He makes no implicit criticism of the employee even though making subassemblies may not have been a good response to the lack of productivity. The coach has helped the employee think that other alternatives might be considered, one of which might be a consultation with the coach. The coach helps the employee think about customers rather than just getting his job done. The coach does slip in a conclusion, but the conclusion is a broad one which still focuses on overall company objectives and he looks for the employee's agreement to make sure of her acceptance.

Good questions ask for thought

Does the coach ask a question that may lead in a poor direction? (We will tackle the availability problem first.) Does he have to answer the supply problem first? Maybe not. But he decided better of that question and asked another which looks like it got him further on to the issue of looking at customer and company goals rather than just looking at supply problems. The coach sneaks in an answer to his own question but he checks to see if his employee is in agreement. Do you think his employee now has a better picture of what responsibility and authority he has for the next time this situation comes up? Does this employee still have something to learn about action and responsibility?

The advantage of asking questions over telling people what they should be doing is very important. Your question about what could be done can lead down a blind alley but telling a person to perform something can lead to a serious difficulty. Questions, however, allow both the questioner and the answerer to examine the answer to see if it is appropriate to the situation. If an employee gives an answer that is not a reasonable response to the situation, the coach can try a new question. The unreasonable answer may be a result of an unreasonable question or an unreasonable understanding of the situation. The question helps unmask that incongruity. Directives, unfortunately, do not always allow the same examination of the situation. Giving an unreasonable direction does not catch itself until the unreasonable consequences (mistakes) have been discovered. Bad questions can be changed quickly. Bad actions take a lot longer to clean up and change.

Should you always know the answer to a question before you ask it? Like all dilemmas that help people learn to think, the answer is: It depends. Stumbling while you look for an answer to your own question has made many a manager/coach feel awkward and at a loss for words. Well, uh, I was just seeing if you had thought ahead and come up with a possible response to the situation. Or: Harrumph, I asked you the question first. Both are answers seen in business comedies and really unnecessary for the coach. Instead honesty is the best response: I don't have an answer to that question myself. We can start looking for the answer together by remembering what happened. In this situation, being prepared to begin the problem solving process is the answer the coach can be ready for.

Still, are there times when you should have the answer to your question before you ask it. Certainly when you are asking your employee to demonstrate that they know established company policy; that they know the basics of mechanical, electrical; or any process theory that they and you should know; or something you have helped them learn in a previous problem solving situation. But try not to be hard on yourself, or your employee, when the foibles of forgetting manage to rob either of you of your memory. After all, we are human and our brains do not follow the rules of perfection that are the inventions of other compulsive people. Coaching can accept errors of memory when some managers are too stuffy to. By allowing errors of memory instead of demanding perfection, coaching helps to create an atmosphere where blame for those errors is eliminated and so the embarrassment of forgetting does not create an unnecessary threat.

Unfortunately though, there is always the risk that an employee will decide to put you in your place by getting mad at you for not knowing the answer to the question you asked and putting you in your place with your dunce cap in the idiot's corner. Yes, employees who have not recognized that creating a threat-free environment goes both for the employee and the coach, may try to turn the tables on you. In their minds, you as the coach must operate error free even though they may not be able to. They may express resentment from previous managers who bullied them. Or they may feel that in your effort to eliminate threat, you now cannot use intimidation and retaliation to protect yourself from their anxiety or anger so it is open season on threatening their boss.

Coaching does not generate automatic applause

Your response is another question: It is time for both of us to cool off isn't it? If he expresses more anger, hold up your hand, palm forward and say: We are still friends are we not? Note here that even though you have not allowed yourself to express anger, your employee will assume you are angry too (and you are likely to be angry until you learn to practice self control in these situations) but a coach in this situation does not coach well by creating more fear but by eliminating fear and the mistakes fear can generate.

How Does a Coach Work through Unfamiliar Territory?

Employees will always manage to take you into unfamiliar territory and you should expected that to happen on a regular basis: Gosh Boss, it happened so fast, I could not do a thing. Or: It is Bill's fault. He laid it on my desk all messed up and would not do anything about it. Requiring an employee to make specific decisions or changes in unfamiliar situations could present insurmountable difficulties for those employees who are not able to think through problems. The key for the coach is to recognize the unfamiliar as a true learning opportunity: Where do you think we should begin?

Ask your employee to compare his and your approach: How do you understand it? This is how I understand it…

Is this how you understand it? Another approach could be: I have not heard this kind of explanation before. Can you fill me in a little more, please? After the explanation, follow up with: Previously I have looked at it as… What differences do you see between our two approaches? Which might be the more promising approach? Why do you think so?

An attempt to reconcile differences between your knowledge and your employee's could be stated: Where do you see points of contact between our two approaches? Or: Which approach gets better results as you see it? Or: What will we have to do to compare the two approaches? Perhaps: What will we have to find out in order to choose one approach over the other? As you learn from your employee, help her learn from you. If you meet something that looks difficult ask: What were the steps you took to make it through this the last time you tried it? Do you see any differences in this situation that we will have to respect? Mental preparation can be superior to learning through action for some people. But if the two of you do a good analysis with a ready plan B you could both learn something. Meeting a new problem is a learning opportunity rather than a situation to automatically avoid.

Mistakes lead to learning, not failure

How Do You Coach When an Employee Tries a Change That Fails?

Remember the problem solving process that you both worked through? You have watched your employee consider several alternatives before choosing the change he wanted to make. You have watched him as he explored the possibility that the alternative he chose might fail and so you asked him to make plans to deal with that failure. Hopefully you encouraged him to evaluate his progress frequently as he walked through the action steps. Evaluating progress frequently should allow him to catch the failure early before too much damage has been done. Now he needs to asses whether his back-up plan should be implemented or thought through again. Consider this conversation:

C: You suggested and I agreed it was worth a try to add more time to the X process to see if it saved time further on in production. How is it working out?

E: Does not look like it saves any time at all; in fact it looks like it makes things worse. (Describes)

C: Are things so bad you want to stop now?

E: No, we can fix things fairly easily but that takes time, too.

C: What were some of the other ideas you considered?

E: (Describes several additional ideas including one that adds a compound during the X process instead of later as a Y application)

C: Looks like there are several possibilities here including getting some more data on your original idea.

E: Yes, I am going to try it a couple of times more but the more I think about it, the more it looks like the added time is not the answer.

C: Why not?

E: (Explains)

C: So what else might help?

E: Maybe if we add time we should get the X process to accomplish more, such as (explains including adding the compound).

C: Looks like adding the other compound is a good plan B candidate. How many times do you need to do it with more time before you decide to try your other plan?

E: No idea right now.

C: OK. Give that some thought. And how will you really know that more time by itself is really not the answer?

E: (Explains)…

This kind of a situation will help you both learn what it takes to create a workable plan B or implement one he created. It is likely you both will see a number of plan B's in your experience together.

WHERE DO YOU FIND THE EXTRA TIME TO COACH?

Asking questions while exploring how someone might do something does take more time than just directing how something should be done. But what happens when an employee does not implement your directions very well? (That is one of the most common complaints managers make about their employees.) You then find yourself spending time trying to undo what was done incorrectly and redirecting your employee to follow your directions more carefully. So the process of directing takes its own kind of time: less time at the front end but more at the end. What coaching avoids are the results of the failure to follow directions. By ensuring that thought goes into a process before the mistakes are made, coaching saves the cleanup time necessary to rectify the mistake. That is one of the reasons coaching is becoming more adopted in today's business climate.

Coaching really does not take more time. The time invested is roughly the same. It is an issue of when you spend your time and the results you achieve with your time. It will take some time to learn new coaching skills. Those skills will initially seem strange but as you master them your coaching skills will make some of your old habits feel strange and outmoded. When you get to that point you will recognize how important it was for you to make the decision to become a coaching manager.

JUST ASKING AN EMPLOYEE TO CHANGE CAN CREATE FEAR

Almost any change you ask an employee to make can create fear. Many employees feel the fear before they evaluate whether or not they will be able to handle the change. But what if he can not do it? The ultimate fear for most employees is the fear they might lose their job. Where will he find another job? How will he pay the bills while he looks for another job? See how working for change can scare people? Few people look at losing a job as an opportunity to find a job with more responsibility and more income. Their fear can be so powerful that an employee might become so afraid to perform his job functions they will lose initiative.

As a coach, when you ask employees to make a change, your first task is to help them see they can handle the change. Ask them to think about each step involved in making the change. Then help them determine that they can make the change. Finish your conversation with: When you start making the change, if you run into any trouble or question, tell me, agreed?

Learning can foster fear

HOW DO YOU COACH WHEN YOU THINK SOMEONE IS MAKING EXCUSES AND DOES NOT WANT TO PUT IN THE EFFORT?

Excuses are always possible when employees are afraid of something. Their fears are likely to be real when you start coaching them as they will not be familiar with how you are going to support them. Sadly, most employees have been trained by themselves to be suspicious of your motives, mistrustful of your support and unwilling to take chances or speak their mind. You will have to convince your employees those expectations should be different now. Changing their expectations will take time and effective coaching.

As you become more familiar with each other, though, those times of fear should diminish. And the employee should become more comfortable about telling you their fears so they can be addressed before an excuse becomes necessary. Anytime an employee gives an excuse, suspect fear and follow up with: Does some part of this look tough to you? Seek to find whatever aspect(s) of your request raises the prospect of fear. Avoid calling it a fear. Refer to it as uncomfortable or difficult as those feelings are perceived to be easier to overcome than fears. Ask: What about it looks uncomfortable to you?

How Do You Work with an Employee Who Is Unable to Change?

The inability to change covers several issues: Lack of understanding of what and how to do it, physical ability, motivation and/or experience. Employees may or may not have tried to change. But that fact is unimportant. It is how you approach the task of coaching them that makes the difference. The approach to coaching these individuals is roughly the same as the person who makes excuses: Ask them to look at themselves in an effort to determine what kinds of reasons they can come up with to explain their inability. Most will say they do not know: Because if they knew, they would have fixed the problem! Eliminate the possibility of an excuse before you launch into a process of trying to assess the real reason behind their inability.

It is possible they may not know themselves well enough to specify what their difficulties might be. In such a situation you must ask them to look at each possibility to help them determine what the difficulty could be. A possible conversation:

> C: You have not been able to make X happen. Do you understand why the change is necessary?
>
> E: Yes.
>
> C: Would you agree that you have tried but been unable to achieve the change?
>
> E: Yes, I have tried but just have not been able to do it.
>
> C: What have you thought might be behind your inability?
>
> E: Darned if I know. I think I understand what you are asking.

C: Have you thought it through in your mind and watched yourself perform each step of the new routine?

E: No. I have only seen myself being able to accomplish it.

C: Well, that is a start, what do you see yourself doing.

E: (Describes, congratulating himself for doing what was asked.)

C: Great. So you can see yourself having done what is needed?

E: Yes. It feels good but not like I really have done it because I have never really done it right.

C: How do you know you have never done it right?

E: It never looks right, it never feels (describes possible correct feelings) right, nobody ever says it's right. I am just all confused.

C: You said: It never looked right, when was that?

E: Remember the time we had to assemble that new machine?

C: Yes.

E: I followed the directions and it just did not look like it was going to work.

C: Describe how it looked please.

E: The cutters were on top of each other and I just knew they would interfere with each other.

C: Is that what really happened?

E: Yea. I had to ask Sam to do it for me.

C: Did Sam explain to you how he got it to work.

E: Nah, I had to leave and I never got around to it.

C: It could help to ask him now.

E: Doubt it, this is different.

C: OK, so you have never had someone show you what needs to be done in a situation like this?

E: No, I do not think so.

C: We will get someone to show you and then you can tell me exactly how it is done. OK?

E: Sure, thanks.

The key to this issue is the how-it-looked. Other reasons for inaction could be: no directions, too heavy, too hard (motivation) or never been done. Once the reason is specified, the proper help can be found. In addition, a coach sees that the employee has mastered the situation. Or it may be determined that a second person is necessary for certain tasks.

COACHING MAY FOSTER COMPETITION AMONG YOUR EMPLOYEES

The process of coaching changes your relationships with your employees. Rather than treating them all the same you will come to see them as individuals. As individuals you will treat them all differently as they will have their own goals and needs. Some will work very diligently to meet their job goals and work harder for advancement or come to your office more frequently while others will take a more patient or nonchalant approach to learning, preferring to work on their own or engaging in more frequent discussions with co-workers. Differences in time spent, number of meetings in your office and their discussions among themselves about what you talk about and how you encourage each person will become apparent. Those differences may lead to a sense of suspicion, alienation, jealousy and even greed between your employees leading to covert feelings of loss and competition. Time with the boss may appear to be favoritism. Those feelings may fester and in turn lead to anger, put downs, or may silent or open arguments and conflict which may impair cooperation and team work.

As a coach, you must be aware of these possibilities. Your employees will likely be embarrassed that such weaknesses interfere with their sense of cooperation and so will avoid discussing them with you. Consequently you need to be on the lookout for any breakdown in teamwork or any hint of estrangement among your employees. Sometimes just checking with individuals can help you work out differences. A possible conversation:

C: You and John have been taking a similar approach to improving production. Have the two of you been sharing ideas?

E: We have been talking about it but I cannot get any real details out of him.

C: Have you been fairly descriptive with him about your ideas?

E: Yes. I do not understand why he does not share with me more and I have got to the point where I am reluctant to even talk to him.

C: Sounds like you have not talked about what is happening between you either.

E: No. He just acts different than he used to. He used to tell me about some books he was reading but he does not even do that any more.

C: Any ideas why? Is he tired or bored or preoccupied with something?

E: I do not know but it is getting irritating.

C: Maybe if you mentioned you would appreciate a comment on what you have shared with him, he would open up.

E: I tried that and he just looked away from me.

C: Have you tried asking for a specific comment on one of your ideas? That might do it.

E: Actually, I think he is stealing my ideas. I heard he was bucking to take the opening in another department

C: That is a promotion is it not? Have you thought about putting your name in?

E: Yea. But he has more experience and a degree. I would never get it.

C: Have you been learning more from him than you think he has from you?

E: I do not think so. I think we have learned the same amount from each other.

C: Does he know you know he is interested in the other opening?

E: We have never mentioned it. How should I start talking about it?

C: Just tell him you heard about it and that you are wondering if he has heard about it, too?

E: Yea. That at least will get a conversation started maybe.

C: Let me know if it works.

Note that the coach opens the conversation with a question that could go either way: Yes, there is sharing and so there is no real issue or a question about the way it actually transpired. He may have had a suspicion that the two workers were not getting along but he wanted to check out his impression before getting further into the possible differences. That is a true coach's approach, rather than just jumping into the issue with: Is it true that you and John are not speaking to each other now?

The coach tries several approaches to help his employee recover communication with John. The coach recognizes but does not open up the subject of jealousy or competition. Instead he helps his employee to discover a way of working out whatever issue might be behind the change in their relationship. Helping them find common ground should get their communication started again.

Coaching turns fear into direction

COACHING CAN CREATE CONFLICT

Coaching tries to resolve conflict but it may create it as well. The coach usually asks questions in most of her discussions. And the coach encourages her employees to take responsibility for what they should do. Sometimes different employees may take responsibility for making changes that may compete for the same resources or try to resolve an issue in opposing ways. At times helping opposing views reconcile will be all that is necessary to resolve the conflict. Look for common ground where the goals of each side are respected through acknowledging the value of each side while both use a share of the available resources.

There are other times when a simple conflict may erupt into deep resentment between people. It is during these times that the coach needs to be directive rather than reflective. Dealing with open angry conflict still follows the approach of finding common ground. The coaching intervention begins with a request that those who are arguing stop talking and face away from each other. Study this conversation between a coach and her team members:

> C: Thanks for getting a hold of yourselves. Relax. What you are arguing about now is unimportant. Put the argument out of your mind. Ask yourself to think about a conversation in which you were able to resolve something important with each other. Remember how you felt then? You were part of a team which was working hard to solve a problem and you helped each other find the answers. You smiled and thanked the other person for their help. Think now about what the other person wants to accomplish. Find two ways in which you can help him. When you have found the ways to help him raise your hand.

(Silence. After both have raised their hand): Are you ready to talk in a helping manner to the other person? If you can, turn and give the OK sign, shake hands, give each other a smile. (After both give the OK sign): Now turn and shake hands. Now the smile. Who wants to start with your helping suggestions? Give one at a time and alternate. Do not respond to the suggestions until you have given both of your ideas.

E1 & E2: (Each gives their ideas.)

C: Now take one idea and tell how that will help. (After both respond to the one idea): Do you think you can carry on your discussion now?

E1 & E2: Yes.

C: Great. Can I leave you on your own or do you want me to stick around?

Note: If the silent time takes more than 5 minutes, or if either cannot carry on their discussion after giving their helping ideas, ask the employees to come into your office and ask them to sit down. Repeat the exercise.

Resolving conflicts that have not reached the level of angry expression follow much the same process as described here. Recognize the conflict is not progressing toward a resolution of the issue. Ask the participants to stop their discussion and proceed with helping them rediscover how they have helped each other in a previous situation then go on to the helping exercise.

Questions to Ask Yourself

- Why do I want to become a coach?
- Do I lose my ability to control what goes on in my department if I coach rather than direct?
- Can I ask questions well enough to maintain control in my department?
- Is maintaining control a necessary part of my job as a manager and coach?
- Is questioning really a game where I say I am giving responsibility to my employees when I am really maintaining control myself but disguising it?
- Do I have the ability to challenge everyone who works for me successfully to make the changes they need to make?

- Do I understand what the true risks of coaching are?
- Do I understand what the true benefits of coaching are?
- Can I tell when an employee truly wants to improve their job performance?
- Can I be a good coach if other managers do not practice coaching?
- Do I have my boss' commitment to support me as a coach?
- Do those who report to me want me to be a coach or do they want me to remain the manager I am now?
- Do I want to be a better manager in my present position or am I trying to be a coach so I can advance in responsibility?
- Do I have the skills to coach in a situation which I do not completely understand?
- What will I do if some of my employees do not cooperate with me as a coach?
- If I ask a question that does not get any positive response, do I know where to go from there?
- How do I finesse getting stuck in unfamiliar territory?
- How do I help someone who has failed to create a successful change?
- How do I help someone who is afraid of change?
- Can I recognize the person who does not want to change?
- Do I understand why conflict resolution must change the focus of the discussion from accusations to helping?
- Could I step in between any of my direct reports and handle a conflict?

RESOURCES

This is an excellent article which gives an objective point of view about coaching:

> *The Very Real Dangers of Executive Coaching*, Harvard Business Review, 2002, pp. 86.

5

Know to Whom You Are Talking

Coaching employs a collaborative rather than a directive management style. Many managers today are directive rather than collaborative either because it is the only style they know or because they do not have the necessary perspective and skills to work in a collaborative way. Others possess a management style that fails to incorporate helping their employees learn better skills, preferring to let people do their jobs except when they make mistakes. Either method of managing still focuses on the job rather than on the employee.

Focusing on the job instead of the person can raise more business problems than it solves. When project objectives are not met, mechanical and technical processes are often suspected as the culprits rather than people issues. If people problems are suspected it can be a capable but imperfect employee who may be reprimanded or let go rather than the manager who does not recognize the need to grow the talent she manages. That approach to management usually results in a higher rate of waste and turnover. Coaching seeks to eliminate that cost, preferring to invest the down time of firing an employee into the down time of achieving work improvement. Work improvement retains the value of the worker in place and the manager's effort within the company rather than allowing the value of an experienced employee to walk out the door.

Coaching, then, is a value added approach to management. The question is: value added to what? The answer is: value added to the attitudes and skills of your employees. Coaching is an effort to orient and train employees to be more effective in their present and future positions. Their true value however will only be realized when they do a better job of problem solving, create more effective teams and move to more responsible positions. Sometimes it may be necessary to hire new people, but improving your people has been shown to have a better rate of return than filling vacancies.

Coaching starts adding value when you tackle attitudes that limit productivity.

ATTITUDES HAVE AN IMPORTANT INFLUENCE ON WORK OUTPUT

Work attitude is usually a very important determinant of the ability of an employee to contribute his work effort. But it can be difficult for a coach to determine what the employee's attitude might be and how that attitude either adds or detracts from his productivity. Some attitudes an employee may harbor about work include:

- Leave me alone: I know what I am doing and interruptions bother me.

- The opposite: The manager better tell me everything I need to know about the job because I do not welcome the responsibility of figuring it out myself.

- I love my job but I hate the people; they just get in my way.

- Do not make me do anything extra because you only pay me to do the basic job.

- Do not make me work overtime; I want to leave on-time.

- I will be angry with you if you do not give me overtime because I need the money.

- My private life is more important than my job so I will use work time to handle personal issues.

- Do not ask me to do more; I have only two work speeds, slow and stopped.

- Do not give me deadlines; they make me nervous and limit my creativity.

- People do better when they enjoy their job so I am going to have fun and I am going to make sure everyone else has fun, no matter what my job needs me to do.

- Everybody else is just a mess; they do not do their job and they will not listen to me when I have a suggestion so nuts to them all.

- The rest of the crew here is just lazy and they will not do things my way.

- I know how to do my job but everything about this place bothers me to the point that getting my work done is impossible.

The list could go on. But you know the general problem. Some people have attitudes that interfere with their productivity. But they usually do not express them unless their attitudes are threatened or they need a reason (excuse) to justify their failures. Do not assume you know an individual's true work attitude is even though they may have expressed one or more negative attitudes to you. People usually have several, as work attitudes change moment to moment depending upon the specific irritant or frustration an individual feels at a particular time. Never indicate that you are disappointed with a person's attitudes or suggest that he change them.

Individuals are responsible for their attitudes; you are not. After all it is their attitude, not yours. People like their attitudes because they are a basic part of how they see themselves and a fundamental part of their emotional make up. To change an attitude takes more than a demand from you that people change. They will not (and most cannot) change an important part of themselves just because you say to or to keep a job. Most people would rather give up their present job and look for another job that would allow them to keep their basic attitudes.

Coaching turns negative into positive

How does a coach deal with these issues: Observe the lapse in productivity, sympathize with their difficulties and frustrations and then channel their work effort into more positive directions through your questions. For example: I can see how that bothers you. What do you think could be done about it? If you were successful, you could put all that behind you. And if you were not as successful as you want to be at least you would have some experience that would give you an advantage the next time you had to deal with it. Would that not be worth your effort? Those questions could focus a person who can look at things fairly positively. A more openly negative person would take less sympathy and a more confrontation approach. A potential conversation:

C: Have you kept track of your tardiness for the last 3 days?

E: No, I thought I got here on-time a couple of those days.

C: Well, we do ask people to be stewards of their own time and productivity. Can my questioning your tardiness help us see how you perceive your importance to our work?

E: I do not understand what you mean.

C: Well, I have tried to call your attention to the fact that you may not have been here an adequate amount of time and so you have not given us the necessary attention we might expect from someone who is as important to meeting our deadline as yourself.

E: It was only a couple of minutes. You really think that is important, do you?

C: Is it a question of time that we are talking about or is it a question of helping you and me understand your contribution to our production goals?

E: Now you have really got me confused. I thought we were talking about an insignificant amount of time.

C: Thanks for helping me understand your perspective. I was wondering if your absence was something that concerned you about your ability to make timely input to your team.

E: I did not miss any meetings. Now I think you are just trying to bug me over some insignificant little thing.

C: Please understand, the amount of time you missed is not the issue. Do you see that if someone was not able to get the input they needed from you, that lack of input may have interfered with your team's productivity?

E: Nobody said they missed me so I think you are just inventing something to make me look bad.

C: I am sorry you see it that way. I am not trying to say you are a terrible person and you made everyone be late. I agree something like that did not happen. I am seeking your understanding of an important principal that your continued commitment to be here is an important part of your job so you can be available when people need your input.

E: It seems to me that you have created a mountain out of a mole hill.

C: Was it I that was late or you? Are we not looking to assess the impact of your tardiness and how it might impact the productivity of your project?

E: And I am trying to tell you that the impact was really nothing.

C: This time maybe. But what about at other times?

E: My little tardiness will not be anything important then either.

C: How do you know that?

E: Nobody ever talks to me when I just get in.

C: Are you sure that will always be the case or might there be a time when an emergency will require your input and you will not be here to respond to it?

E: Now I know you are making a mountain out of a molehill.

C: Are molehills never important?

E: No.

C: Help is never small when it is needed.

E: I still do not see your point.

C: It is not my point that we are talking about. It is your tardiness and its consequences that we are talking about. Do you continually wish to ignore your responsibility to your colleagues? Do they need your input on a timely fashion? And can you make your input if you are not here?

E: They can leave me a message and I will respond to it when I get here.

C: Is that really good enough for you to be perceived as a dedicated member of your team?

E: If you tell them I am no good then they will probably believe you because you are the boss.

C: So up to this point you have failed to see that you are responsible for how people see and interpret your behavior and your willingness to be a timely contributing member of the team?

E: You really want me to believe that I am a bad person, right?

C: No. I am not trying to make you out to be a bad person. I am asking you to view your behavior from someone else's point of view rather than your own so you can see the value that people give to your timely contributions. Do you see yourself as valuable?

E: Yes, otherwise I would not work here.

C: Yes, we see your value too. I am asking if you could only make yourself more valuable by being here when others need you.

E: Why did you not say that in the first place?

C: Well, are you willing to get here on-time so people can use your valuable input?

E: I guess so.

C: You are either going to be here or not. What is it? Yes or no?

E: I guess I had better say yes.

C: Is it a question of saying so or being here?

E: There you go again, I said yes.

C: And do you mean what you say?

E: Yes.

C: Good. Your colleagues and I appreciate that.

This conversation may look like a lot of crowing for a little gain. Or is it? How often do people seek to avoid responsibility for their self-centered behavior? Usually as often as they can! And, if they can successfully avoid responsibility, what is the possibility that they will change? You know the answer to that question. It may take a lot of time and effort to help people commit to making a change in their behavior and to allow them to be more positive and respectful of their responsibilities to their job. It may take several challenges to your point of view before an employee understands he cannot put off his responsibility. Once people have learned to look at the consequences of their behavior, the chances are they will be willing to make the change more quickly when the situation demands. And they will be aware that your questions will keep coming until they make a commitment to change.

The person who was late may be late again. But he should be aware that you will ask him to evaluate his behavior again, much in the same light with much the same result. Your task is defined as: Keep the responsibility where it belongs, within the person, no matter how much they seek to pass it off to you or a co-worker by blaming you for being unreasonable and punitive or anything that is plainly negative. You must ask him continually to accept the responsibility for the change that the situation of the job demands. And you need to help him realize that it is never just a question of saying but it is a question of commitment to putting the change into effect. Once he commits to the change he can and will be reminded that he has made a commitment so he will be held accountable if he does not follow through. A possible conversation:

C: Are you aware that you have been late again?

E: No one said anything.

C: I am saying it now.

E: No.

C: Well you were and I was told by someone who needed your input that you were not here.

E: They did not tell me about it.

C: It does not matter that they did not tell you. The issue is you made a commitment to be here to make timely input to your team and you have not followed through.

E: I was on-time for months and no one said thank you. Now I mess up one little time and you are all over me.

C: My intention is not to make you feel bad or to ignore your being on-time. My intention is to ask you if your commitment to be on-time is still a solid commitment. Or is it merely a when-you-want-to-be-here commitment?

E: I said I was going to be here.

C: Yes and you were not. What does your absence mean?

E: I had something important to do.

C: Does the fact that you had something important to do for yourself excuse you from your responsibility to your team?

E: It was an emergency.

C: Does a personal emergency excuse you from your responsibility to your team?

E: You really do not like me do you?

C: It is not a question of whether I or anyone else likes you. It is a question of your commitment to your responsibility to your team. Your tardiness suggests you are not committed. Is that the message you want to send everyone and me?

E: No.

C: How should it be handled when you are not here again when you are needed?

E: Leave me a message.

C: Have we been through this discussion before?

E: I do not remember it.

C: Well we have discussed the fact that a note does not make up for you not being here when your team needs you. And you made a commitment to being here. Apparently when you make a commitment to change you do not intend to honor your commitment. Is that true?

E: There you go trying to put words in my mouth again.

C: I am not trying to put words in your mouth. You made a commitment to be here. I and your team accepted your commitment. You did not follow through. Are we to assume that your commitments are worthless?

E: You are trying to make me into a bad person again?

C: You may think so but is it possible that you are trying to say that worthless commitments should be acceptable from you and anyone else? How would we get work done on-time if everyone here made worthless commitments to our projects? You really want to get our project done do you not?

E: Yes.

C: Good, then how should we respond to you when your commitment to get the project done is not honored and you do not show up on-time?

E: Will you want to fire me?

C: No. I will not want to but will it be necessary?

E: I guess I better be here.

C: Yes, you said it again.

The subject of this conversation, being on-time or tardiness, is really incidental. The same conversation can be had about any of the attitudes mentioned above. Just substitute the problem and the same conversation is possible. The change in his perception from passing it off as unimportant to the perception that a change is necessary comes when he says yes. Yes to the fact that he is valuable and that he wants to get the project finished. When an employee agrees to those ideas, he has committed himself to making the change and recommitted himself when he is found to have been unable to make the change. You must seek his commitment to positive actions because a person will only commit themselves to something they perceive as being positive. Committing to something positive must be shown to be preferable to allowing something negative otherwise he has committed himself to something negative, an admission that no logical person could allow herself to make.

Coaching changes excuses into commitment

Also, when someone is asked to recommit himself to a change, he must be confronted with the issue of how his omission should be considered the second time. Reasonable people know that they only have so many chances to prove themselves. You must allow them to believe that negative consequences will absolutely follow before the next omission or commission. Without the perception of the negative consequence, the motivation to continue the positive change will not be there. It is the question: Do you really want…? That maintains the responsibility of honoring the answer in the employee and removes the onus from you of making the observation. As long as the employee answers the question positively, he remains responsible for the consequences of his answer and his behavior, not you. The moment you ask an employee to please change his behavior, you become the responsible person (you want it badly so it is your problem now) and so remove the responsibility from the employee. (All you have to do boss is not care and things will be OK.) Moral: Questions put the responsibility where it must reside, on the person who must answer with appropriate behavior.

ATTITUDES WILL INFLUENCE HOW YOUR EMPLOYEES REACT TO YOUR COACHING

Attitudes make a difference in how employees approach their job. Their attitudes about you and how you work with them also make a difference in how they see you and work with you. What possible attitudes might exist regarding your management, and in particular your approach to coaching?

- You may think you can quiz me about how I should do things but you really cannot because you already know the answers.
- Just tell me what you want me to do; do not waste my time with questions. Leave the work to me.
- You are supposed to give answers; I thought you were the boss?
- Your questions confuse me; I do not know what you want.
- Why waste time with all these questions? What answer do you want me to give you?
- If I do not know the answers to your questions, how can I learn anything unless you give me the answers?
- You hide behind all these questions. How do I know I can trust you to really know what I want to say?
- No one else around here acts like you do.
- All your questions do is make me work harder. I never know what you want.
- I can come up with a lot of answers but none of them ever seem to satisfy you because you just ask more questions.
- You tell me you want me to learn and I want to but how can I learn something if I do not already know the answer to your questions?
- I bet your boss does not like you asking all these questions; I told him it just wastes time and he agreed.

- I think and think when you ask me a question but I do not think I learn very much from your questions.

- You say I should try new things on the job but I do not want to do anything different; it is just fine the way I do it now.

- I am not sure I trust you when you say I should try new things. What happens if I try something and you tell me I have made a bad mistake?

- I do not think this company wants anyone to do anything differently; I talk to other people and they tell me this improvement stuff is bunk.

- I do not want to be a manger, why should I spend my time and effort to do better at my job?

- You tell me you want me to learn so I can be eligible for more challenging jobs. It takes so long to get promoted; it just is not worth the effort.

- I wanted to take a course to learn some things and the company turned me down. This business about learning is a farce. It takes too long to learn on the job. It is easier to learn what I have to by listening to real experts.

- You just want me to admit that I am wrong.

There are likely more negative attitudes than these regarding how you manage and ask questions. Notice what seems to be common among them: Confusion as to the true direction you are trying to encourage people; doubt that the extra time and effort of coaching and questioning will result in real personal gains; doubt that you have the employee's interest instead of your own at heart; and doubt that the company wants you to try this new management style.

Coaching changes confusion into direction

The confusion and doubt harbored by an employee reflect the average person's reasons for not embracing just about anything different or new in life. Keep those two issues in your mind as you coach. Clear up any confusion and find out what the individual needs to experience or what could turn doubt into certainty and comfort to allow her to embrace change and learning. A possible conversation to handle confusion:

C: I sense you could be confused about something.

E: You are right; I do not understand why you are asking me all these questions all of the sudden.

C: I understand that changes that are not explained can be confusing. I have tried to ask more questions and apparently you are wondering why I am doing that. Is that a fair statement of what you are trying to find out?

E: Yea. Why are you asking all these questions?

C: Let me know if this clears up the confusion. I learned that asking questions can focus a person to learn more about what the question is trying to find out? Does that make sense so far?

E: Not really.

C: Well, did I say anything that you understood even a little bit?

E: Yea. It helps to learn if you ask questions.

C: Exactly. Questions put you on a path to explore something.

E: But I still do not understand why you ask questions.

C: OK. Do you know everything there is to know about your job?

E: Pretty much.

C: Pretty much. Does that mean you know absolutely everything?

E: Well, not everything.

C: OK. On second thought it appears you remembered something.

E: Yea. I am not sure about XYZ.

C: OK. What do you want to know about it?

This conversation starts with a question that is not posed as a question. Many people would not answer a direct question about being confused (Are you confused?) with an affirmative because being confused is not a positive condition and they would hesitate to admit it. However, if a coach indicates that she sees something but is not sure what it might be, the employee does not have to admit something negative and can instead admit to something positive such as looking for an answer. The initial statement includes a maybe so the coach's observation can be denied if the employee feels uncomfortable about admitting his confusion: I am glad you do not feel confused; I just wanted to check out if I could help. Now something negative has been changed into something positive.

THREE IMPORTANT OBSERVATIONS

Three other observations about this conversation are important. It includes several guesses on the part of the coach about the employee. Making good guesses about what you think is going on in an individual is an important part of being a good coach. You are constantly observing how the person is acting and talking. From those observations you try to infer if there are issues that the employee needs help with (but may not be admitting to himself or you) and are important enough for you to try to resolve. However, try never to act as if you know for sure what is going on in the individual because you might be wrong. Your guess is always couched as an effort to help because that is what a coach does, help where needed. Your guess just tries to find where the help could be focused.

The second item to observe is that the coach admits it is one of her behaviors that leads to the employee's confusion. Your guess and your admission that it is something you did that leads to the confusion shows that you are possibly wrong and not the employee. Remember, by admitting that the responsibility for a mistake or problem can be yours, a coach tries to keep the ego of the employee strong and in place. That is important because a person who feels comfortable will be more open to changes and learning. A person who feels confused is reluctant to take on changes because he is afraid the change will cause more confusion.

There are times when a coach will want to challenge the strength of an unbending refusal to change because a person who is strong in denial will not open his mind enough to admit a needed change. You saw that situation in the first conversation on page 39. The key to opening the crack in the denial is to show that the denial is inconsistent with a positive value that the individual holds at the same time. The key to helping the employee change in that conversation was the observation by the coach of the possibility that the person believed that he should be excused but others should not be.

Notice in that first conversation how often the employee denied that anything was wrong with his attitude. The coach's part of that conversation consisted of attempts to find an inconsistency that would allow her to present that inconsistency to the employee in a manner that would be undeniable to the employee. The inconsistency has to come out of a present conversation because any attempt by the coach to point to an inconsistency in another conversation can readily be denied as a false understanding by the employee. Finding the inconsistency and resolving it is the key to personal change.

Good learners look for the inconsistency in themselves and then find out how to resolve it. When you find a good learner you can support his desire to make personal changes. He can be responsible for defining any change that he sees may be necessary and making that change for himself. He may want your help but he is responsible for his own growth. Your goal is to help all of your employees understand how inconsistencies can focus their learning. When each of your employees takes that responsibility for herself, you will know your efforts to coach have paid important dividends.

CONFUSION AND DOUBT

The third item to observe in the last conversation is how close confusion and doubt are to each other. Any confusion may plant doubt. Not being certain grows doubt and doubt can result in debilitating fear. So as you deal with a stated doubt, try to treat it as confusion. Confusion is easier to change than doubt.

Coaching changes doubt to direction

People may doubt something positive will come out of their efforts. That doubt may stop them from making an effort to move forward. But if they see their doubt as a confusion of goals that needs to be clarified, finding out exactly what the different goals or paths to the goal are will erase the confusion and remove the doubt at the same time. A possible conversation:

E: You want me to take on this new process. It is brand new; I have never seen anything like it and it looks to me like I would take forever to master it.

C: What is there about this new process that looks confusing to you?

E: I do not know. I look at it and I am not sure how to get from input to output.

C: I hear you. Little seems to make sense and you are afraid you will not get the hang of it fast enough.?

E: Yea. I just do not see that I will be able to master it in the time we have to get it running right.

C: Well is there any part of it you do understand?

E: Yea, the part where the two machines are linked together. I have seen it before so I do understand it. I just do not see how it connects with the feeding and processing parts.

C: Well, if you were to do it, how would you do it?

E: (Describes how he would separate and organize the processes.)

C: Why would you do it that way?

E: (Explains why.)

C: Well, it appears you understand the physics and chemistry of what should happen. Does the new process respect those principles?

E: Well I have not looked at it that way yet.

C: How have you looked at it?

E: Just as if I have seen the same mechanisms.

C: In what other ways can they be looked at?

E: I do not know how the parts are connected, how the liquid and solid flows work, and temperature additions and subtractions.

C: OK. What way would make the most sense to you?

E: I guess temperature additions and subtractions.

C: What should it look like from that point of view?

E: (Describes.)

C: What kind of time will it take for you to analyze it from that point of view?

E: A couple days.

C: When is our go/no-go/must decide date?

E: A couple days.

C: Will you have time to look at some of the other ways to analyze it if your preferred way does not work?

E: No idea.

C: What chance of figuring the situation out before our decide date do you think you have? Is it any better now that we have talked than you thought a few minutes ago?

E: Yea. Pretty good.

C: What is clearer now that you did not understand before we talked?

E: A place to start and a place to go if it does not work the first time.

C: Good. Keep me posted if you are ready to try.

Notice the relationship between confusion and a block to action. Notice also that the coach does not immediately try to point the employee to explore the physics of the process as a means of clearing up the confusion. The coach sees the connection to physics and mentions it in general but as the employee did not mention it, the coach pursues the conversation trying to find other clarifying connections that may help the employee. It is the employee who mentions the clarifying concept that is eventually encouraged.

In this conversation, time is a block that is successfully addressed. The employee is not only blocked because of his lack of understanding; he is also blocked because he does not believe that he has available time to explore the new process before production has to be resumed. The coach helps the employee see that, even though the time is short, it looks as if there is enough flexibility in the time available to look at the process from several points of view. The employee comes to see that he has a place to start and a place to go if the first approach does not work out. The coach asks the employee to explain his approach so the coach and the employee know what the operational approach to be tried will be.

There is one coaching misstep in this conversation. Can you spot it? In his third statement from the end, the coach asks two questions instead of one. He is not sure what the employee sees as pretty good but he gets away with it. Asking two questions usually means that the responder will take the question that is the easiest to answer while the other question goes unanswered. By asking two questions the coach loses direction and may waste time while the responder goes his merry way dealing with potentially irrelevant issues. In this example, the questions are not that different so the pretty good response can be taken as an answer to both questions. Usually people ask two questions because they sense the first one is not what they want to ask, so they change the question. If you want to ask another question, say the first question is not what you want to ask then rephrase the question the way you want it mentioning: What I really want to ask is….

Notice also that the coach does not respond to the employee by asking what is stopping him. Instead the coach responds by asking the employee to address the confusion of his situation. Many people see confusion as acceptable because a lot of the world can be confusing to just about anybody, so being confused is not necessarily a super bad problem that one has to deny. But the work situation demands action so stopping work because of a block is less acceptable and many employees will not admit they are blocked. However, most will admit they are confused. So the effective coach starts with a question that opens up the acceptable confusion issue and never uses the concept of block. The employee may perceive the situation as a block. In fact this employee sees that he can not get from part A to part B so he is addressing a block without using the concept. The employee owns the confusion rather than blaming it on the process. That is why this conversation reaches a conclusion fairly quickly. If the employee blames the process as being too complicated or impossible, the coach has the responsibility of opening up the employee to the fact that he is responsible for dealing with the issue no matter how difficult the process might be. The coach, though, reminds the employee that he will help her think the situation through.

A Coaching Approach to the Know-it-all and Other Marginal Employees

The occasional employee claims he can do anything and everything. When you hear that claim, ask the employee to justify it. But do it in an inquisitive and not in a doubting manner. Ask for situations where he has used his skill and what his success was. Ask for his explanation about how he learned it: school, hobby, helping a friend, armed services or other experience. What limitations might he put on his abilities? Does he feel his experience fits his present responsibilities? How might he know he was too optimistic in believing his experience would work well in any situation? Ask him to write about his experience and put it in his file. Your actions and questions confirm your interest because if he is right, his skills may be useful in yet unknown situations.

Others forget they have a skill because it has been a while since they used it. Ask each employee to explore her past experience and write down what she might have an interest in doing. Put that write-up in the employee's file and your mind. Interests provide many opportunities to exercise creativity. People who create usually respond willingly to a challenge.

Unfortunately, others try to hide their skills because they want to limit the amount of work you ask them to do. Even though they might be responsible for making a change they will usually do it reluctantly. Ask them what economy of effort they will accomplish by making a change. Help them understand that taking the trouble to adopt something new will save effort in the long run and might even result in a promotion. Helping them explore the benefits of change may open up their willingness to be creative.

Over time, you should come to understand which of your employees takes less or more responsibility for their performance and learning. Keep track of the level of their refusal to accept responsibility by seeing how often they try to blame you or their co-workers for mistakes and how they deal with their problems. Your skills in opening them up to their responsibilities will show in the number of times they deny them or project them onto other people. As you gain skills as a coach, you should be able to help people fear criticism less so they can face responsibilities and deal with them directly and in a more efficient and effective manner.

People Learn in Different Ways

The primary way that most of us learn is by watching how others do things. Then we copy what they do. Some people are very astute observers, being aware of every little thing while others are not very precise in their observations. As a coach you will encourage people to learn from others where possible. You will check on their observations to determine if they are accurate and you will learn quickly which individuals do a good job of observing. Ask the person to describe what they observed and if he is prepared to reproduce the other person's actions. If he is not prepared, either ask if he needs to observe more or if he wants verbally to describe and write down the sequence of what he would do. You can check his description and if you find discrepancies either ask him to consider them or ask him to think through the action steps again.

Learning is done in different ways at different times

After correct behavior has been observed, the next step is to learn it. Learning means incorporating the behavior into existing abilities so it is repeatable without the presence of the example. The ways in which different people incorporate their observations and descriptions of how to do things are also variable and should be known by a coach who encourages learning. Different ways people learn have been described as immersion, pragmatic, reflective or theoretical. These different ways begin with pure action repetition with the immersion person increasing in thought to the predominantly theoretical person. David Kolb in *Experiential Learning* described several learning dimensions.

The immersion people develop their behavior primarily by repetition. They prefer to be immersed in the activity of doing and rehearsing what they want to learn. Sometimes they want to have the person from whom they are learning around longer than other learning styles. But they practice what they should learn until they know they can reproduce what they need to do consistently. Their end goal is an emotional confidence that they know they can do what they need to change and will not be criticized in their activity. A coach can help these people by finding opportunities to practice the change.

The pragmatic people learn best when they can see and understand the practicality of the behavior. They are motivated by knowing that rewards will be achieved when they learn something. They may change their basic behavior so they can do it more quickly or more easily by making some adjustments. They often make some adaptations to their basic behavior but their adaptations are usually minor until they have had extensive experience. They primarily want to know that they are doing something with a purpose. But when their purpose has changed, their motivation to learn and continue their work can be lost while they look for another purpose. Your best help for the pragmatic people will be to help them explore how the change makes things better and why they should adopt it.

The reflective people like to take time to think things over. They will try things in their mind and can be somewhat cautious before they begin to try the behavior that they are to learn. They may watch the model person and look to see if that person has a consistent process or if the model has some variations that could be adopted. When the reflective people have these questions answered then, and only then, might they try their hand at the new behavior. They have trouble with deadlines and seldom will respond positively to an external pressure to learn. These people may have had trouble in school so they have developed a strongly independent approach to learning. Also, they may be hindered in their learning by knowing that they will be watched and graded in their behavior. As a coach you can help them best by questioning where they are in being comfortable with the change and reviewing with them the sequences they consider adequate.

The theoretical people are high on thinking about and low on trying new behaviors. They can be very creative in abstracting from their experiences in observing. They may adopt none or few of the behaviors they have observed from their example. In fact, they may not even want to watch someone else do what they need to learn. They may concentrate on looking at the raw material going into the process they need to learn and examine the finished product carefully, then construct in their mind what they need to do to work through the steps to arrive at the final product. Theoretical people are often engineers, physicists or very physically skilled people who are challenged by the task of doing something completely different than anyone else might do it. They might be inventors and may be reluctant to do anything that is repetitive. Your help will be best focused on thinking through the process with them until they become willing to try it

What Is in It for Me?

These four types of learners respond to their inner strengths. They relate primarily to how they have learned previously and find it very difficult to learn something new in a different way. There is a fifth group of learners who are not primarily motivated by past experience but instead pays more attention to the rewards offered from their environment. These people want to know what is in it for them. They do respond to awards, medals and bonuses as long as they are given quickly after they have successfully learned the new task. They pride themselves in being highly adaptive and maintain that they will do anything if the price is right. Unfortunately, they do not have very much staying power. Once they have mastered something they want to move on to the next situation especially if they can get more rewards from the new opportunity. Salespeople often are externally motivated and fit this type of learning style. An effective coaching style with this type of person is to help them find their next reward while helping them polish their skills in achieving it.

The challenge to you as a coach is to understand what style an individual employs and to help him adopt the demands of the situation to how he is most comfortable in changing and learning. Good questions here include asking a person to explore how he likes to learn while helping him examine his limitations or efficiencies in learning. Some employees may be quick learners in simple situations but may reach a limit or find a situation where they cannot improve themselves and so will need considerable direction from their coach. Others will not want much oversight by their coach but will want to choose their own methods of changing and refuse to observe time goals and deadlines. Others may rely on promises and trickery to make you think they are changing and learning. The coach must know which employee is which. Be prepared for surprises. Some will change styles just when you think you know them. Still others will surprise you with their independence from your efforts to help once they learn they are really responsible to face challenges.

As the demands of the situation change, the learning behavior and success of the individual will change. Check in with the individual on a regular basis to see how they are adapting to the new situation and if they feel in control or are lost and confused. Help them find their next possible step.

COACHING APPROACHES TO THE STRESS OF TIME AND CRITICISM

Time stress will be the most important negative determinant of learning for most of your employees. Help them be aware of how their perception of time might be threatening them, or if they truly have the skills to be in control.

Questions to ask when you see time stress include: What have you tried to move things along? What kind of help do you need? Can I help you get over the hump? Are you feeling tired and need a break? Will that help or only compound the problem? Do you know what you need to resolve in order to feel better, and confident you are going to make it? When will things get critical (and/or difficult) for you? What has to happen in order for you to get through this crunch?

Critical for the coach will be how your employees respond to your efforts. If they remain in time stress after your coaching session they may begin to criticize your coaching efforts as ineffective and perhaps even begin to see you as ineffective or, even worse, perceive you and your coaching as dumb and stupid. When their comments get personal you need to look further into the make-up of your employees. They may belong to any of the following types: the avoider; the frustrated yes-man; the procrastinator; oversensitive to time pressure or criticism; or respond to stress by arguing about irrelevant issues.

The moment the avoider becomes aware of a deadline or receives some criticism, no matter how slight, he responds by acting as if the deadline or criticism is not important. He may deny their importance to the extent that he forgets entirely that the deadline or criticism have any relevance to what he is doing. Recognizing either creates anxiety and the anxiety interferes with his focus and commitment.

No matter how you ask the avoider to process the looming deadline or the significance of the criticism you will always get the same answer: What, me worry? Respond by asking for a short outline of what changes he has made to accommodate himself to either situation. Usually the avoider will give a very cursory response which lacks insight into the need to change what he is doing. Accompany your request for analysis by adding: I am here to help you get this issue behind you so you can be comfortable that you are adequately dealing with the situation. How do you see the deadline (criticism) influencing how you do your job? Does it help to really think about something now so you do not have to worry about it again when things are going well? Do your part and I will do mine.

There are some employees who depend upon a boss describing exactly what they need to do in order to feel they can do an acceptable job. They may procrastinate making any change until they get instructions and/or a demonstration. They are a type of avoider (they do not want to worry about deadlines and criticism either) but they usually feel that if they find out exactly what is expected of them, everything will work out well. They will become frustrated when they realize that they do not have adequate answers to your questions or in responding to an examination of their adequacy in following directions. Help them find a resource that will help them to their comfort level if they feel frustrated or uncomfortable following your questions.

Frustrated yes-men will always turn your questions back to you and ask you to answer your questions for them. They may fail to understand what the fuss to change is all about. They may plead that they have always done what you told them to do and request another description of how things should be done. When asked to analyze how they might do something, they plead ignorance, or explain they have never been asked to do something like you are requesting, or they are sure if they do it according to their present understanding, they will do it wrong.

These people need your assurance that they have been adequate in the past and you are certain they will do adequately in the future. What is standing in the way is their lack of an attempt to try the change out. Help them see that a mistake will not get them fired but they must make an attempt in order to get the feel of what needs to be changed and you will be there to help them analyze what they were able to accomplish.

Coaching fosters independence

As they might be successful in spite of themselves, mention: Certainly you will be pleased if you were able to do it yourself? Think of how good it would feel if you could actually do it on your own. Or they may be overly self-critical. Help them see that practice which helps them understand how to perform is the key to gaining self-confidence and you will assist them in thinking through and evaluating their success.

The procrastinators do not need anyone to remind them that time is wasting. They already know they are late but have all kinds of excuses that interfere with getting on with things. Ask each one to share their thoughts about possible failure, certain difficulties, and just plain distaste for the task they are postponing. Ask them to think through the reality of each hindrance and help them prepare a response to the failure and difficulty. Help them savor the good feelings of a job completed as a substitute for their distaste.

Several repetitions of these sessions will help activate their desire for success. Procrastinators want you to know exactly what their perceived hindrance is. As you deal with one, another one will mysteriously pop-up and another until you give up because they have too. They will use the stress of time as an excuse too because the stress of a deadline is perceived to be too overwhelming. Responsibility in time is your best tool. If the change is not made in time, consequences will occur. Make sure they know them and that you or the company will impose them, excuses or not. You may even have to threaten to eliminate your help and leave them on their own if they do not finish the job quickly. After all: I have to move on to others who also need my help.

The overly sensitive individuals are the opposite of the avoiders. They belong to the procrastinator class because they believe complaining about things is really working on the change task, whereas in reality they are only putting off something unpleasant. Help them understand their fears and anxiety and help them see their irrationality in a similar way you would work through with the procrastinator: deadlines and consequences.

ATTITUDES MAY CHANGE AFTER AN EMPLOYEE BECOMES AWARE HE HAS MADE A MISTAKE

Some employees know they make mistakes and take that fact in stride. They make the necessary change and go on. If it is a mistake that they cannot change before it affects someone else, they admit the mistake, apologize and correct the consequences.

There are others, however, who are afraid of the consequences of a mistake and try to hide them by denying or not owning up to their ownership of it (them). Others may hide the mistake because they are ashamed, expecting better of themselves or believing that others look down on them too. As a coach, it is not necessary to be aware of the different emotions that may be behind the cover up. But you have a bigger issue to address now because of the mistake, its consequences and the cover-up needs to be dealt with.

Deal with the consequences first. They are visible. Help the person who is dealing with the consequences do a good job of cleaning up. Fixing the situation is your first priority. Do not worry now about who made the mistake and what should be done to avoid the situation again. Those issues become the subject of coaching and analysis after the consequences are rectified. In this way the customer (inside or outside the company) is happier because business can move on with minimal time and effort expended while they wait for your product. Customers know that any delay could be the result of a mistake. Knowing what the mistake was will not be helpful to them, but letting them know the delay came from learning a process that will speed things up in the future will help them appreciate your efforts and look positively toward the next time. Your employee should help customers deal with the consequences of his delay. Rather than just promising there will be no next time, though, he should mention the new way of how things will be done. A change in place builds confidence that promises lack.

Clean up consequences first

Make sure that all of your employees know the order in which the consequences of a mistake should be dealt with: Fix the consequences, find out where the consequences came from and then explore what fix needs to be installed so that the consequences do not happen again. Then ask if anyone learned from that process. Make sure you get some learning from everyone involved. Knowing who the person was who made the mistake now becomes irrelevant. You congratulate your team on rising to the occasion and the situation becomes positive for everyone and no one becomes the scapegoat. Mistakes become easier to deal with because everyone is working on them and an individual does not have to be afraid of losing their job or finding out they do not really know the situation very well because they have been a part of learning what to do when anyone in your group makes a mistake. Everyone will learn how to deal with and avoid the same problems. So cover-ups are not necessary. Cover-ups may still happen because guilty people may need lots of experience that cleaning up is more important than blaming people. They may still blame themselves but that is a problem for a counselor rather than a coach.

It would be more helpful if you explain your pragmatic approach to mistakes before one is discovered. That way you can get your team moving more quickly when one is discovered. If you do not have everyone familiar and comfortable with the process, however, make sure you review it with as many as possible before the next mistake shows up.

Questions to Ask Yourself

- Why is it important to focus on the individual instead of the job?
- How do attitudes affect how an employee works?
- What kinds of attitudes do I need to know?
- How do I work with attitudes?
- How can I be certain an employee is committed to his job?
- What good is job commitment anyway?
- What is the difference between confusion on the job and doubt?
- How does a coach deal with them?
- How do I help different types of learners improve their job skills?
- How do I coach all the different kind of people who are my employees?

RESOURCES

While somewhat dated, this book is a classic in its field; it explains not only the theory but the practice as well of how people learn.

Experiential Learning, Prentice Hall, 1984

www.bestmanagementarticles.com. This Website has many discussions of positive management behaviors.

6

Coaching Approaches to Communication Issues

A large telecommunications company asked their managers: What are your most difficult business challenges today? About two-thirds of the respondents listed communication as one of the top three challenges. When asked for the top challenge, communication was mentioned by more than half. Perhaps half listed communications as their most difficult problem because another study at a Fortune 500 company showed that half of all communication efforts are perceived as failures. That is a lot of wasted time and effort. Think of what you could save if your communications were right on the money the first time!

So what seems to be at the bottom of the communications problem? When asked: What about communication seems to be the most difficult? Few can really be specific but the consensus challenge seems to be: getting the message across. When asked to expand on what that means, a list of communications situations are cited, including:

- People seem to take things any way they want to.
- I did not really understand what he wanted.
- I could never get my question answered.
- The meeting broke up and I did not really understand what I was supposed to do.

- I did what I thought was necessary.

- I do not know why it was not good enough.

So the challenge of getting the message across appears to mean: Do I know if the message really got through? Other managers express something similar: I say something but am never really sure the other person understands what I say, the way I intend it to mean. This chapter deals with the challenges a coach faces in getting her messages across as intended.

WHAT IS COMMUNICATION?

Communication is a need (idea) put into words and gestures that the sender believes will trigger a response in the receiving person which corresponds to the intent of the sender. There are four parts of this definition:

1. sender

2. message

3. receiver

4. feedback

The sender is the person who creates the message and has the need. The message looks at the receiver as a resource to handle the need and carries a description of that need. Questions clarify that need by asking for information or learning. The receiver responds to the need by giving feedback.

Communication highlights a need

Remember Marshal McLuen's famous statement: "The medium is the message?" What he meant by that is the words are only part of the message. How the message is carried is more important than the words. Coaches have taken that concept to heart and learned that the process of communicating is often more important than the content of the words used. Questions we will address include:

1. Why do we usually prefer to communicate face-to-face?

2. How does the sender structure her message so it is received with clarity and trust by the receiver?

3. How can the receiver get a clear message so he responds to the sender's real need and not only to his (the receiver's) needs?

4. How must feedback be structured so that the communications loop is completed?

Why Face-to-face?

Speaking allows a more complete message to be delivered than writing or even a video. Facial expressions, voice tone and other non-verbal cues add to the message and contribute to communication efficiency. Next to words, facial expressions carry more meaning than voice tone. It has been estimated that facial expressions carry 40 percent of a message's meaning. The primary limitation to personal speaking is the distance you can cover. Video conferences can help cover long distances easily, but video does not allow people to shake hands in greetings or agreement so is limited in its ability to carry meaning between people. Video can also be misleading because the strength of the visual medium can overwhelm the meaning of the underlying communication, even blocking it out. Remember Nixon's poor showing in the televised debate with Kennedy that has been blamed for his election defeat? Face-to-face communication is crucial to the coach as actions mean more than words.

Ways that face-to-face communication carries meaning include:

1. You can feel the situation. If you suspect something in an e-mail or phone conversation, the immediacy of the in-person conversation may give more evidence of their level of urgency and commitment and allows the parties to confront the reality of the situation more adequately.

2. Complex cooperation issues can be worked out. The give and take of people in each other's presence is often necessary to get commitment to complex action plans. Objections or other reactions can be responded to quickly by explanations and further reactions. Supporting evidence can readily be brought into the discussion through argument or reasoning.

3. A leader can project his personality and show his enthusiasm. You can swear in a letter and shout on the phone but those media still attenuate the emotional aspects of their messages. In personal

encounters, on the other hand, gestures and voice level carry the emotional meaning more completely.

4. Commitment can be assessed more adequately. Seeing is believing. The reason to communicate is to get something done about the problem. Being with a person can give a firmer understanding of the level of commitment and urgency in dealing with the original need. When you are in the same room and the receiver says: I will get right on it. The sender can see how the receiver turns to get started. Of course, the receiver can also lie to the sender's face. Lying can happen in any medium, but it is harder in person and the sender can always use the immediacy of the situation to confront the receiver with that lie.

Hidden Meanings Inherent in Sender Messages

Sending clear messages can be difficult because of the many silent variables that impact a message's meaning. Messages can carry a threat or a sense of support from the sender to the receiver depending upon how the message is phrased.

Judgment/Support

A message always communicates a need. But different needs can have vastly different values. The value expressed in the message depends upon the importance of the need and a sense of how urgently the sender needs it. The value part of a message is communicated whether we are aware of it or not as it is inherent in the existence of the need. For example, consider a mother involved in searching for her small child after a tornado destroys part of their house. She calls (with or without a tremor in her voice): Tommy, where are you? A weak voice responds from under the rubble: Mommy I did not do it. We do not know how mischievous the child normally was or how judgmental the mother had been in other situations, but her question shows how difficult it is to communicate in a situation without showing how important an answer is to the sender.

Speech is so often judgmental in business that defensive responses can be regularly given in non-judgmental situations simply out of habit. If people are not able to respond in a manner that removes the threat of the situation for the sender, each succeeding communication will increase the sender's and receiver's basic feeling of insecurity. The deeper the insecurity, the more an individual is likely to blame others for the uneasiness of their situation and the more likely they are to distort communications by making evaluative judgments about those who communicate with them. Why did you not call? This may not be intended to be judgmental, merely looking for explanatory facts; but almost anytime the word why starts a question, it can be received as a criticism of the receiver.

In contrast to evaluative speech, descriptive speech tends to arouse a minimum of threat. Requests for information, or presentations of feelings, perceptions, events, or processes which do not imply that the receiver needs to change his behavior, create a minimum of threat. As opposed to creating a threatening climate, description creates a supportive climate. Descriptions allow the receiver to concentrate on the situation and on its obvious merits without adding the emotional threat of the sender to their situation and response. Another way of asking the why-did-you-not-call question in a less judgmental way is: Was there something that interfered with you calling?

> There are six additional communication variables where threat or support can be implied:
>
> | Threat Climate | Supportive Climate |
> | --- | --- |
> | Dominance | Collaborative problem solving |
> | Manipulative | Spontaneous |
> | Ignoring | Empathic |
> | Authoritarian | Participative |
> | Certainty | Explorative |
> | Fear | Control |

Dominance/Collaboration

Communications which are used to control the receiver through domination regularly evoke resistance. In most of our business interactions the sender is trying to get the receiver to do something: to change an attitude, buy a product, influence someone else or agree not to do something. The degree of the domination of the communication depends on the honesty and openness of the effort. Hidden motives suspected but not specified in the message constitute a threat to the receiver as they may be surprised by the communication and so could have little idea of how to adequately respond to those motives.

Implicit in attempts to dominate another person is the message that the
receiver is inadequate to the situation. If you must be told how to do things,
the inherent message is that you are inadequate for you must be ignorant,
uninformed, immature, on the losing side, lazy or unable somehow to make
your own decisions about how to respond to this message. It is no wonder
then, that dominance in management induces defensive reactions in the
message receiver. There is no other way to do it, is there? This is not perceived
as a true question but a domineering criticism of the receiver.

Needs are not answered by threats

A problem solving orientation is the supportive opposite of domination.
When the sender communicates a desire to collaborate by defining a mutual
problem or a problem he perceives the receiver might want to improve on,
a climate of mutual support is developed. That climate is further developed
when the collaboration extends to the resolution of the mutual situation.
Collaboration tends to communicate that the sender has no predetermined
solution, attitude, or method to impose on the receiver. Collaboration
and problem solving allow the receiver to set his own goals, make his own
decisions, and determine his own progress relative to the problem at hand.
Questions also help to alleviate dominance in a message: What do you think
will be necessary? This is preferable to the no-other-way attitude.

Manipulative/Spontaneous

Senders who are perceived as using others for their own ends threaten
receivers. Information may be left out or falsified, or secrets may be kept by
the sender. If the receiver suspects manipulation, whether true or not, he may
interpret the situation as a threat and respond with a lack of cooperation or
plain resentment which will likely obscure his response. You better find that
out! This appears manipulative and threatening.

On the other hand, senders who are perceived as spontaneous and non-
manipulative may receive straightforward listening reception. The perception
of spontaneity is enhanced when the receiver sees the sender make
appropriate responses to the receiver's need without any attempt to forcibly
modify or negotiate them. A coach's spontaneous support goes a long way to

establish a good communications climate. That is terrific! This is spontaneous and supportive.

Ignoring/Empathy

No one likes to be ignored. People desire to be seen as having value through being asked for their help and involvement. Once a person feels her skills are ignored, she may respond in future situations with less than enthusiastic cooperation. You cannot possibly be serious! This shows the person has no value and so will likely be ignored.

Showing empathy for receivers and their situations will hopefully create in the receiver openness to the sender's situation. Allowing the receiver to practice his skills to help allows the receiver to feel good and accepted. Empathy is an important part in building the supportive and trusting climate for successful communications. Yes, I know how tough that can be! This shows empathy and support and is one of the coach's most important communications.

Authoritarian/Participative

Authoritarian messages emphasize the difference in status between the sender and receiver. The authoritarian sender tries to impress the lowly receiver with the sender's importance, whether his situation deserves it or not. When nits are elevated to crises by a sender, the receiver reacts with aversion and disgust. The receiver may respond to the letter of the request, but his level of enthusiasm will be less than optimal. A sender acting as a superior and meeting jealousy in a receiver may find sabotage as a result. You think you have something better? This usually gets a silent response: I just do what they tell me and I do not care what happens.

Alternately, the sender who seeks to share perspectives, resources, priorities and results with the receiver has a better chance of receiving cooperation and enthusiasm. There may be real differences in talent, ability, financial worth, appearance, political or business status and power. If these are not employed to force the responder to focus on his lower status, but the skills and attributes possessed by the receiver are used to mutual benefit by the sender, the receiver will feel supported rather than threatened. Then the receiver will generally attach little importance to the status distinctions, but instead will identify with the supportive aspects of the communication and be more inclined toward cooperation. If we work together, that will really make a difference! This emphasizes the participative and supportive intentions of the co-worker or coach.

Certainty/Explorative

Those senders who think they know everything create a threatening climate for receivers who may indeed know what the sender should know. Those who seem to know the answers communicate to the receiver that he is not needed except as a puppet to carry out orders. Dogmatic senders communicate they need to win the argument rather than resolve their need situation. Indeed, know-it-alls often create communications situations merely to impress receivers about how good they are in everything including communications. Unfortunately, know-it-all's communicate nothing as most receivers in that situation stop listening. What other answer could there possibly be! This is closed and threatening and is not on the coach's list of usable comments.

To create a supportive climate, the sender must communicate that she is willing to try new things, explore different ideas or perhaps even change her own attitude about the situation. The sender who communicates the tentative quality of his analysis will also communicate his problem solving needs. If the receiver is allowed to have some input into the definition of the situation, the sender is structuring a supportive rather than a threatening climate. Should we give it a try to see how it works out? This shows the coach's interest in and support of learning on the job.

The sender can doom his communication to failure by creating an unbending, threatening or disinterested climate for the receiver. Unfortunately the sender cannot guarantee communication success by creating an explorative climate, but it greatly helps.

RECEIVER BLOCKS TO COMMUNICATION

A coach must be alert to the several ways a receiver can make it difficult for a message to get through:

- Screen out the sender when the needs expressed do not coincide with the receiver's ideas, selfish motives or negative attitudes about work.
- Hear their expectations only. Many receivers guess what the message is

going to be and are often wrong but still impose their own meaning or become confused.

- Ignore benefits the sender uses to enlist support of his need.
- Misinterpret the message when meanings of words differ.
- Respond before the message is complete and so miss crucial parts.
- Cloud the message in emotion of fear, disdain, or confusion.
- Respond only to parts of the message in an effort to ignore needs they are not sympathetic with.
- Evade the intent of the message believing the receiver does not deserve and his needs be met. Evasion through lies rather than rebellion is the usual response.

The burden of communication is clearly on the sender. Most often, it is the sender's needs which have prompted the message. He must do all he can to facilitate creating a supportive climate and in helping the receiver understand how a positive response is possible for the receiver and may benefit her. When the sender is fixated on his own needs as to forget the receiver's needs and attitudes, the communication is doomed. However, where the receiver has an obligation to respond, she should honor the sender's situation enough to question the value of his need. In an atmosphere of mutual support, the message can be negotiated. What are your bets about the success of a message sent in an atmosphere of threat? Thus it is necessary for the coach to operate in a climate of support.

SKILLS FOR EFFECTIVE RECEIVING

A coach must be sensitive to how her questions and messages are understood. She must look for several responses in her employees to assess that her questions and communications have been correctly received:

- Suspend judgment through openness to the need;
- attentive listening;
- questions about what might be unclear;
- an admission of emotions that may cloud the message;
- an attempt to negotiate differences; and
- feedback that demonstrates understanding and buy-in to the need.

These skills may be difficult to perceive as the receiver responds. In any case the coach needs to ask for the receiver's analysis and reaction, assessing his understanding by asking for a summary or paraphrase of her communication and looking for responsible action. If the employee cannot state the original message the coach should work with the employee to develop these skills so understanding and buy-in can be improved.

Questions to determine openness include: Do you understand my need? Does my need seem reasonable? Is there anything that might interfere with you getting that done? What have you been thinking as we talked?

Listening makes great conversation

Questions to determine listening include: Did I put you to sleep? Did I ask my question so it was understandable? Have I said how much I appreciate your attention to this matter?

Questions about clarity include: Is anything unclear? Have I confused you in any way? Do I need to restate anything?

Questions or comments about emotions include: That kind of a situation seems uncalled for. How are we doing? Something like that would bother me—how are you doing with it? Is there anything in what we have discussed that bothers you? As you think about this is there anything that you cannot live with?

Questions about negotiating differences include: Have I said anything you disagree with? Is there anything in this situation that you find unacceptable? Are there differences here we need to reconcile?

Questions about feedback and buy-in include: What do you think about this situation? What similar experience have you had? Does my question meet with your expectations? Can you give this your undivided attention? Is there anything standing in your way to working with me on this? Tell me as completely as you can how you see what I am asking.

There are general comments and questions the coach can make and ask as well: How do you think we connect when we try to communicate? I am always trying to improve my communications, do you have any comments you might want to make about how I communicate? You seem to work hard at communicating; do you have any secrets for me about how you do it so well? How are we doing? Do you think I need to watch for something that needs improving? By coaching receptivity to your coaching questions, you can help improve openness to everyone's communication needs.

WHAT ABOUT NON-VERBAL COMMUNICATION?

As you can see most communication is like an iceberg; only a small part of the whole communication lies above the surface in the words exchanged. Sometimes hand and facial gestures help carry the conviction and intention from the receiver to the sender. The possibilities of what can be communicated non-verbally are as vast as there are the number of looks and moves. You might want to consult a book on non-verbal communication to help you understand this issue.

It is important for senders and receivers to know, however, that each of us has non-verbal habits. Each of us should know the gestures we use and what they communicate. That way we can warn others not to mistake a smile for a please-do-not-be-disappointed but no, instead of a yes. If you are not aware of how you communicate non-verbally ask other people to comment on the gestures they see you use and what they think you may mean. You might be surprised to discover you are giving gesture messages that contradict what you say.

HOW FEEDBACK WORKS

Feedback comes in two forms: 1) Your message is not clear and 2) I understand your need and will handle it for you. Any other kind of response is not feedback. The response may be an outright denial of the sender's need or an attempt to change the sender's need to one that the receiver can agree with. It is a common misconception by almost everyone that making any comment to the sender is feedback about the sender's message. Often a response is only the receiver's perception of what he wants to do without knowing whether his response will work for the sender or not. That misconception can lead to long drawn-out discussions that never arrive at a conclusion. A possible conversation:

E1: Would you please hand me the X?

E2: Wait a moment.

E1: I need it now.

E2: Just a minute; hold your horses.

E1: What are you doing that you cannot get it for me?

E2: I have to get something done.

E1: How long do I have to wait?

E2: Until I get this thing into the X.

E1: That could take forever.

E2: No not long.

E1: I will get it myself.

E2: OK.

Notice that E2 did not deny E1's need; he tried to negotiate the time when he would comply with it but rather than be specific about when he would comply he made the exact time of his reply fuzzy. E2 thought he was responding to E1's need but he was only talking about his own situation and never attempted to understand E1's need or give him feedback about his need. Finally E1 arrived at another answer to his need and E2 agreed to allow E1 to let E2 off the hook. E1 realized he would not get the cooperation to handle his need so decided to handle his need himself. Another possible conversation:

Boss: The brochure is the wrong color.

Assistant: The background, the text or one of the pictures?

B: The picture on the back page.

A: There are lots of colors in that picture.

B: I am talking about the whole thing.

A: Do you mean it is too red or blue or just washed out?

B: Too blue.

A: That could be because we used a different kind of film.

B: Well it just does not look right.

A: (Believing he now understands the specific need, the assistant changes to negotiating what he should do about it.) Should I ask the photographer to shoot it again with the other kind of film?

B: That will take too much time. Ask him to make it less blue.

A: How about this other picture; is this blue the way you want it?

B: Yes, ask him to do it that way.

Notice how the assistant clarified the specific need his boss was talking about then suggested a behavior to resolve the need. That alternative was rejected so another solution was proposed which the boss agreed with. This assistant was smart; he knew it might take several tries to get the right blue his boss wanted but he was perceptive enough to provide an example to get to the yes he was looking for from his boss.

Feedback deals with the sender's need; negotiation deals with the approximate ways the receiver proposes to deal with that need. When the need is clear and the receiver proposes a manner of responding to that need that the sender can live with a communication is accomplished and an OK, or Yes, or Let us do it, become the signs of agreement. Without the yes, no communication has been made. Agreeing to disagree is not a real agreement unless the pair commit to working on the need at another time.

As a coach, differentiate between feedback and negotiation: Your response has not helped me so far. Are you agreeing with some of my need but not all of it? I am not sure what you are trying to tell me. Are you saying you do not understand what I need or do not agree with it? Are you trying to negotiate with me about what you will do? Give me some feedback so I can make my need more clear. Your refusal does not tell me what you need in order to help me. If I changed what I was looking for could you help me? What can you give me that will help me out in this situation? Are we negotiating about what you will do for me or what you want from me so you can cooperate? It does not look to me that what you are willing to do meets my need. Would you agree?

Get to the yes, but be careful that the agreement be built on a solid promise that the value of the response will meet the value of the need. Many disappointments and business mistakes and failures lurk behind an inadequate response to a well-stated need. Feedback is not just any response to a need request. Yes and I am not sure what you are asking for are feedback. Any other response is a negotiation heading toward a partial agreement or defining the rewards the sender might bestow for compliance.

The Sender and Receiver Are Both Responsible for Communication

Blaming someone else about communication glitches gets the pair of you nowhere. If a communication fails, it is the responsibility of both parties to acknowledge the problem, examine why it happened and discuss changes in your communication that will eliminate the lack of agreement. Pledge to each other that each of you will work to improve your message sending and reception. That pledge will help to create the necessary trust for better communication.

Use Jargon Carefully

Jargon is communication shorthand. It can save time if both sender and receiver understand it. If the receiver does not understand the jargon, using it can create uncertainty which can help create a threat climate. Some people are afraid to ask what a word means for fear they will appear stupid. If you even suspect that someone does not understand a word, explain what you mean even if you risk them feeling that the explanation is a waste of time. What hurts more: wasting time, being ignorant about the meaning of a word or the fact that poor communication means a goal is not met?

When in Doubt, Over-communicate

Time is precious to everyone. But making a mistake because of a communication error uses more resources than just time to get things on track again. Remember this rule about getting rid of the noise in your communications: It is cheaper to spend the time now than later. Remember this second rule: Learn where communication errors occur and do whatever is necessary to bring the mistakes to zero. It may take a lot of trial and error to achieve but be assured it will be worth it.

Talk about what it takes to communicate

Help Evaluate Rather than Complain

As a coach you will inevitably encounter a time when your employee did not get your message. Ask them to sit down with you and evaluate what was helpful to you in their response, and what was not. Ask if you could have done anything as the sender to help them with their response. Your effort to take some of the heat for an inadequate response will help create the supportive climate for later communication efforts. Thank them for their efforts to work out communication kinks and ask them to be aware of any suggestions you might use to improve. What is fair for one is fair for both in the communications game.

When Are People Most Apt to Listen Attentively?

Communications research has shown that people are most open to the requests of senders when the receivers themselves need help in dealing with their situations. Make sure you are aware of the employee's needs before you send your own. Making sure the receiver gets attention may uncover that you have similar needs. Similar needs get the best response when they receive similar attention. If you can find someone who shares your need, you can get ready help when you combine your resources.

Beware of the Noise Criticism Can Create

Information critical of others is believed more quickly than positive information about the same person. Negative information needs less confirmation in a person's mind than positive information. People will complain about receiving little help before they will praise someone for any amount of help they have given. When you hear critical noise about a sender or receiver, take time to evaluate what the truth might be before you allow it to mess up the trust that might have been built between you. Do not let a rumor destroy what good communication has created.

Coaches cannot fail to communicate! If an employee does not understand something clearly, he will invent any meaning so he can comfortably exist under the illusion that he really knows what the other person wants, whether it be true or not. To be an effective coach, build solid relationships through clear communications based on untiring support and a thorough knowledge that you and your people communicate effectively.

Few people will start with looking at how they communicate; instead they usually will project their problems and criticism onto others. For most people, they see their own reaction to what others say or do as positive but they do not see or feel how others react to them. Help your employees ask for constructive evaluation from others and assist them to make changes in themselves. Then watch how their meetings improve. A possible conversation about communication:

E: I try and try to get through to my team but most of the time when we get back together, they have no idea what we talked about in our last meeting.

C: Do others express that frustration or are you the only person who feels that way?

E: I don't know, they never say anything to me about it.

C: How about going to each person at their work place, ask if he or she has any hint about how you might improve the way you communicate?

E: What good would that do?

C: Do you think your question might reveal some people have specific issues in understanding you? That might start a conversation where you could talk about what each of you might do to communicate better?

E: (Talks to team members, and returns to coach.) Most everybody said they did not have a problem with me but one said they had problems with me.

C: Good. Did you understand what she was saying and were you able to discuss ways of changing how you communicate with each other?

E: She said I tended to interrupt people and I did not give good examples of what I was talking about.

C: Did she give you good examples of her points?

E: Yea. She reminded me how I interrupted her yesterday and something I said was too complicated, a couple of times the team met last week.

C: If she made sense, what did you learn from her comments?

E: I could not remember when I interrupted her. I never barge right in like that. But I do remember the long statement I made so I tried to think of an example that would make my idea clearer to her. I tried several times and she said she finally understood what I meant.

C: How about if you watch yourself to see if you interrupt anyone. That way you will have a better idea of whether you do it or not.

E: Yea, I could try that.

C: Good. As you tried to help her understand your point from the meeting, did you understand what she was talking about?

E: Not really. I think she does not know the process very well so she blamed her ignorance on me.

C: OK. Is it possible there might be others in the meeting that might not understand what was being discussed?

E: Maybe.

C: If you find out how many do not understand you, perhaps you can make a better effort to explain yourself to them and when they understand you better they might get better ideas about what is being discussed. Possible?

E: I think you are putting all the responsibility on me to communicate again.

C: Actually I am putting the responsibility on you to understand how others see you. It is best to start with ourselves and improve how we come across because it is easier to change yourself and if you change yourself maybe you will not have to change other people to get them to be better communicators.

E: Oh. You mean if I look at how I communicate maybe other people will be able to communicate better with me and we will have better results in our team?

C: That is an excellent insight into how communications can improve.

Questions to Ask Yourself

Sending:

- Do I ask myself about the purpose of my message before I say or send it?
- Do I divide my message into easy to understand parts before I say or send it?
- Do I check myself to see that I have communicated the complete message?
- When the situation requires, do I explain why the message is directed to the particular receiver?
- Do I present why the receiver should be interested in my message?
- Do I speak clearly enough to be heard easily?
- Do I look at the person with whom I am speaking so I can see their reaction easily?
- Do I ever do other things (straighten my desk, etc) while I am sending a message?
- Do I realize what I say is usually only a part of what might be said?
- Am I aware when I am reporting facts as distinguished from reporting value judgments in my communications?
- Do I itemize points to make them clear instead of using general terms such as everybody, always, etc?
- Do I catch myself when I give negative connotations to the behaviors of others?
- Do I adapt my message to the world of the receiver so he can understand it better?
- Do I pull rank when I ask others to help me?
- Do I seek to evaluate rather than criticize?
- Do I use trite expressions rather than exact words when I describe someone?
- Do I realize that different people perceive the same situation differently?

- Do I watch for differences and try to reconcile them or do I let the message receiver grapple with those issues?
- Do I try to create a supportive, trusting climate when I communicate?
- When I sense an agreement do I give the receiver a clear yes?
- As a coach do I communicate threats or support to my receivers and senders?

Feedback:

- Do I show by my attitude that I am glad to have my receiver ask questions?
- Am I happy to have the receiver restate my message to me?
- Am I sensitive to nonverbal gestures and respond well to these silent types of feedback or negotiation?
- When my receivers respond do I contradict them before they have finished?
- Do I get defensive when others challenge my need?
- If the receiver and I differ about my message, how do we work out the differences?
- Do I thank my receiver for their effort to understand my need?
- Do I try to improve my communications by asking others to tell me how I come across to them?
- How do I respond when a receiver does not immediately agree with me?
- Can I sense how close a receiver is to agreeing with my need?
- Do I know the difference between feedback and negotiation about the sender's need?

Receiving:

- Do I try to create an atmosphere free from distractions when I receive?
- Do I let my own thoughts interfere with the sender's message?
- Do I try to understand why they are sending to me?
- Do I demonstrate a receptive attitude when I receive or do I respond with cynicism or indifference?
- Do I check the message I received with the sender to make sure it is the same?
- Do I try to fit the sender's message into context so I know why she is sending to me and what difference my response could make to her?
- When people send to me do they feel that I really understood their ideas and feelings?
- Do I try to refrain from prejudging the value of the sender's message?
- How do I show the sender that I am listening and believe I understand her?
- Am I able to restate the sender's need when his communication is concluded?
- How do I ask for more information?
- Can senders communicate bad news to me or only good news?
- Am I skillful in using listening to gain information, learn, and grow?
- How do I communicate to the sender if I feel he is making an unacceptable request?
- When I feel we are in agreement do I say exactly how I agree to the sender's need?
- If I am able to respond only to a part of the sender's need, how do I communicate that?
- How do I find out when a sender will accept a partial agreement with her need?
- Is it necessary for me to apologize or explain when I cannot respond positively to a sender's need?

- Do I communicate my agreement with a clear yes?
- As a coach am I open to the communications of everyone?

RESOURCES

An excellent primer for learning and mastering communications is:

Essentials of Business Communication; visit *www.westwords.com/guffey* for more information.

Coaching Approaches to Problem Solving Issues

7

Research on problem solving by a number of companies and consultants has shown that seven main issues account for the sources of over 94 percent of the errors made in business problem solving:

1. Failure to set measurable goals to be achieved.

2. Failure to prioritize goals so that the most important goals are not worked on first, wasting time and resources and causing time commitments to be missed.

3. Failure to find the right cause for a problem–also wasting time and resources when inconsequential problems are worked on.

4. Failure to recognize the problem as a new problem and thus failure to come up with a new, inclusive and creative approach.

5. Failure to plan adequately so that complex tasks are not coordinated properly.

6. Failure to be concerned with what could go wrong with action plans and to adopt contingency plans to handle those possibilities–when something comes up people have no plan B to insure progress.

7. Failure to assess accurately what results have been achieved from previous problem solving efforts, so repetition eats up time and resources.

Notice that all seven sources of error have one theme in common: failure to do the specific thing that the situation demanded. As a coach one of your primary responsibilities is to assist your employees do a good job solving problems.

THERE ARE EIGHT STEPS IN WORKING A PROBLEM TO ITS CONCLUSION

1. Analyze the situation:

- Who are you; what is your responsibility, skills, and limits?
- Look at the trend–is the problem getting worse, staying the same or getting better?
- What is the history of the problem and has anything been done about it before?
- Timing–when must the resolution occur: right now, later or much later?
- Impact–is this a little problem or is it big and significant?

Ask the right question at the right time

---

2. Establish goals and prioritize them:

- Out of all the things that are happening now, taking the big problems and the ones that need to be done now, what specifically do you want to accomplish?
- State the goal in measurable terms with a time limit.
- State what you must accomplish as well as what you would like to accomplish.

3. What are the causes of the problem–if you do not know, find them:

- There may be immediate causes, contributory causes and even multiple causes.
- Determine them and decide which ones you can affect. Some you may not be able to deal with.
    - In that case you may have to deal with symptoms, or find a way to ignore the problem.

– Or you may have to experiment to see what you can and can not accomplish.

4. Develop alternatives to handle the problem:

- Be creative here! Do not just respond with the first thing that jumps into your mind.
- Brain Storm! Try to develop several lines of attack. Maybe even reformulate the problem and try again.
- Good problem solvers often develop a dozen or more possible solutions before they find a reasonable approach and start to do something.

5. Choose your best solution and develop an action plan:

- Look at which of your alternatives meets most of your objectives and looks doable.
- Develop a plan of attack that states who will do what, when will they begin, and when will they end.
- Also, what must they contribute to the overall solution so the next person will be able to do their best job.
- Good coordination is a part of a good action plan.

6. Determine what can go wrong with your solution and develop a contingency plan:

- This is where mistakes occur most often. The prime rate goes up, your key worker gets sick, etc.
- Try to imagine those things that could threaten your success. There are many and you will not be able to deal with them all.
- Create contingency plans for the threats that could do the most damage and are the most likely to occur no matter how much damage they could do.

7. Now, perform your action plan.

8. Evaluate how well you did:

- Compare goals with results.
- You may want to establish new goals or adjust your action plan and try again.

Now that you have seen the basic plan, repeat in your mind the eight steps: situation analysis, goals and priorities, causes, alternatives, action plan, threat analysis and contingency plan, implement the plan and evaluate results. Keep these in mind. Remember where you are in the process. Help your employees learn which step they are on. One of your best questions is: Where are you (we) in the problem solving process? Coordination between yourself and your employees will be facilitated by knowing the answer to that question. In this way people will not be trying to solve a problem before they know what the cause is, among other possible process mistakes. Here is a more complete description:

1. Analyze the situation

Who are you? Every problem has to be solved by someone. But not everyone sees the same problem in the same way. The janitor may see a pile of dirt in the corner as a problem needing a broom and dust pan, while the president may see the same pile of dirt as a problem needing a new janitor. You may have spending authority for $500 and need to purchase a $5,000 computer. So how you respond to any situation will be determined by who you are, what your responsibilities and authority limits are, and even by how you feel when the problem is presented to you.

Who you are may be a group of people. Each person may be responsible for only a part of the situation you are facing. It will be helpful for each of you to know the skills and limitations of each participant so you can more easily divide the various responsibilities. You may be the boss with an employee. You may need to see the problem from the other's person's point of view depending if you are the customer or the salesman or the person who just passes problems on to others. The better you know the difference between the points of view of the people involved, the better you will know how the other person will cooperate, or not, and what you might need to do to ensure their cooperation. Sometimes people will want you to take over their problems when you have no responsibility or authority or skills to deal with it. In such a case, helping the person to find the skilled and responsible person may be the way to resolve the situation from your perspective.

Trend

A fire burning out of control is something that has to be dealt with right now because it usually gets worse. Flat sales may wait a while if there are other problems that are more pressing such as high manufacturing rejects or raw material supply problems. Reducing employee turnover cannot really be touched if recruiting or employee interviews cannot be conducted. Seeing how different problems are related helps determine the priorities of issues. But if they are related they may need to be worked on simultaneously.

Remember, every problem has a history, and in that history trends may be embedded. Flat sales may occur just before the summer season and if that is the regular pattern, we know it is not as much of an issue as it might be when flat sales are occurring just before school starts when we know they are supposed to be at their highest for the year. Also, what did we do the last time we had flat sales? Was it successful? Knowing the history of a trend helps determine if the situation needs a quick response and helps to avoid repeated failures or to avoid reinventing the wheel.

Timing

Nothing seems more a factor of business problem solving than time. When have you had enough of it? How much time we have before a solution is needed strongly determines how we can approach a problem. If we are starving now, waiting for the spring to come to plant a crop is not an option as a solution. Sometimes we can perceive where short-term solutions may resolve the problem for the moment, but may not be long-term. Renting an office instead of buying one may fall into that category.

There are times when your real problem is a long-term one but you can only see it as a short-term one. The large profit margins on big cars managed to seduce the American auto manufacturers into a short-term profit solution, ignoring the long-term need to innovate gas efficient models. When they found the American public turning to smaller cars, the manufacturers had none to sell so lost billions more than the large profits on big cars had made them. Sometimes a problem can only have a long-term solution. Getting to the moon took over 10 years of planning and technical innovation before the solution was achieved. It is much better to know how timing will influence a solution when you begin to consider it than to embark upon a solution then find out that results are needed sooner than first thought.

Impact

Certain problems have to be worked on because they are plainly more important than others. Not having any ice cream for dessert is not an important problem for most overweight Americans. Having clothes that fit is usually more important, but avoiding high blood pressure is critical to a person's survival. No gas in the car will keep it from operating as will an engine that does not turn over. But getting gas will not solve the do-not-go problem so fixing the engine may be the bigger problem except in the desert where, if you cannot get gas, you probably ought to let the motor rust while you hike out. In business the big problems have to be dealt with first. Sometimes we fool ourselves into trying to deal with the little problems hoping we can get the time to deal with the big problems. Often what results is little problems keep draining capital so no time or resources are available for the big problems.

Many companies have learned the hard way to put the little issues aside and concentrate on the big issues. If the big issues are not resolved, they will often destroy all the work that has been done on the little ones. That is what separates the big ones from the little ones. Every job has their big and little issues. The president may have bigger ones than you have but you have got your big ones too. Always ask yourself if this problem is related to any other and which are bigger and more important so you can establish priorities in your efforts and coordinate them with others.

What part of the solution are you responsible for?

---

2. Goals

Knowing what you want to accomplish is a very important part of problem solving. If you really do not care what you want to accomplish, just about any kind of a solution will do. Wanting to reach a 20 percent increase in sales this year will require a different strategy than wanting to reach a 50 percent increase.

Goals must be measurable

It is nice to have good employee morale but unless you have a way of measuring it, it may not be worth your while to bother worrying about it. What should you do, count the smiles, or count the grievances, or the turnover rate? If constructing a measure is too difficult, it is better to forget that measure and use the measures that you have. But be careful here too, as sometimes the things we can measure are not really worth measuring. Absentee days may not be as important a measure as the number of cancer cases per thousand man years when you are looking for measures of worker health; but the latter measure is certainly much more difficult to gather data, though it is a specific measure.

There is another very important aspect of defining your goals. Some goals must be accomplished or the effort is a failure, while others are nice to have but if you do not get them you can live without them. Think about these musts and wants as a part of defining your goals. For example, one family with three children might insist that each child have a bedroom for themselves while another family might perceive it acceptable that the oldest child have one and the two younger have one together. Consequently, the first family would insist on a four bedroom home and not look at three bedroom homes, while the other family might accept a three bedroom home but also accept a four bedroom home, everything else being equal. Some business problems are similar: A machine must be able to thread, but if it can thread and slot that is even better while a slotting machine by itself will definitely not do.

When is a goal a real goal? When you know why it is a goal. Buying a machine can be a reasonable day's work for your procurement officer. What the machine should do and how fast and how much it should cost are necessary parts of his goal statement. Why those goals are in place is determined by what your contribution margins are and what your supply commitments demand. Profit, expense savings, time efficiency, community improvement and tax savings are all good basic goals. To get them all, you must be aware of them all. Be sure your goals are rooted in necessary and not just desired objectives.

Priorities

Look at your timing, trend and impact factors and determine which goals you will work on first, second, third, etc. There are no formulas that will mechanically crank out the ranking. If you are going to lean on one factor, that would probably be impact; but even a little problem now that is getting worse needs to be evaluated for its potential future impact. Among those goals that are of equal impact, timing will help to sort out what should be worked on first, second, etc.

3. Cause

Knowing the cause of a problem is the most important single aspect in resolving it. If your gas line is frozen, charging your battery will not get your car started, nor will filling your tank. At times there are multiple factors that combine. There may be a long chain of events that connect to result in the problem. Both these situations require thorough analysis. To handle a problem well, with many cause factors, requires that all the factors are dealt with, starting with the major ones. To handle a problem that is the result of a chain of events requires an analysis that uncovers the link between the causes

There are two key clues to finding a cause for your problem. The first is a search of the events that occurred at the time your problem first surfaced. A new supplier can be the source of spec changes that lead to an increase in product rejects. A new operator not following standard procedure could be the key to increased downtime. In both of those examples, as in many problem cases, a specific change led to the events that surfaced as the problem. Look for relationships between an event and a problem.

The second key is an examination of where you are experiencing the problem and where you might expect to see the same problem but are not. This helps to zero in on a possible explanation while eliminating rival possibilities. Look for those differences in the areas of what the problem is, where it occurred, how long it occurred, and describe its size or proportion. Here is an example:

	Is	Is not
What:	Widget brackets hole off-center	Wuffle brackets oblong holes
Where:	Production line A machines: 3, 7	Production lines B, C machines: 1, 2, 4, 5, 6
When:	Afternoons only since June 1st not everyday	Mornings, night shift before June 1st everyday
Size/Proportion:	Holes are correct size 100 percent of holes off-center	Incorrect size intermittent

An examination of these facts would lead you to look for peculiarities relating to what is happening with machines three and seven in the afternoon. In this real case, the source of the problem was: The summer sun had finally reached the point where it was shining on the control mechanisms of the two machines leading them to short-out because of the heat and resulting in improper drill guidance. A shade over the window solved the problem. Note that the key was when the problem took place, leading to the understanding that the machine itself was not the cause but it was something happening to the machine at a particular time. A search for events after the June 1st date lead to a blind alley as no operators had changed nor had materials changed (which were the same for all the machines anyway). Nor could any other changes be noted including maintenance. Observance of the sun coming in the window at a particular time on the two machines led to a suspicion of the root cause. But it was not everyday because clouds sometimes obscured the sun.

So cause can be a tough thing to find, but specific data examined rigorously and systematically can help. This problem drove the manufacturing manager crazy for over 3 weeks. Everything on those two machines was changed, including the control mechanisms. After the data was organized, the critical factors of the afternoon and the two machines stood out. A mechanic was detailed to observe the machines during the afternoon, and he observed the sun shining on them. That observation led to the resolution of the problem.

Remember, dealing with the cause is the most effective way of solving your problem. But some causes cannot be directly dealt with even if you do know them. In those situations, you may try to limit the effect of the cause, handle the symptoms like aspirin does a fever, ignore the problem and hope it will take care of itself (like high gasoline prices) or change the way you operate so that the problem does not bother you as much (drive less). To a certain extent, we have already moved our problem solving outline to developing alternatives in dealing with the cause. But knowing how adequately you can deal with a cause is important to estimate here, because recognizing that the real cause cannot be dealt with now will save you a good deal of wasted energy and resources. Your knowledge of your ability to deal with certain causes will depend upon your experience and ability, so take good stock of yourself and your company resources. Resources squandered in dealing with something you cannot handle well means fewer resources available for other problems. Also, a blind alley may require consulting help. Help is usually cheaper than shots in the dark.

Fixing the wrong thing wastes time and resources

---

4. Creating alternatives

Two very important items should be noted here: Do not try just anything simply because it might look promising at first glance then get in the habit of stretching yourself to come up with new answers even for routine issues. Ineffective management sometimes prefers workers to be busy rather than thoughtful. The cry often is: Do not just stand there–earn your salary; do something, forgetting that doing the wrong thing is often worse than doing nothing. Gathering more information is often a reasonable way to respond to a problem.

Problem solving, like being a tennis or golf pro, requires regular exercise and much practice. The best problem solvers are the ones who continually challenge themselves to look for a new way. New ways do not always work, but they generally work better than old ways which have been proven to be only partially effective. Does doing the same thing ever get different results? And when you try new solutions, you continue to build valuable experiences about the process of solving problems as well as building precious confidence that when things get tough, you can come up with the answer. Problem solving requires some risk taking and those who do not take risks never get good, they just collect unemployment pay.

Here is one handy way of generating creative ideas. Pick up a dictionary, randomly pick a page, then stick your finger on the page and open your eyes to read what word it points to. Then sit down and force that idea to suggest a solution to your problem. It is handy, because it never fails to suggest an idea. It is almost foolproof because how that idea fits your problem is up to you; here is an example of how one such session worked.

A group of about 30 homeowners had purchased new homes in a development. All had guarantees for the usual start-up problems complete with forms to file with the developer when something went wrong. The difficulty was, the developer seldom responded to the repair requests and by the time he did, the problems had usually become worse. Group threats, calling him at home at nights, pickets around the sales office and lawyers had not worked to get timely help. The group, in desperation, tried the blind-man's-dictionary technique. The word was overgrown. Yes, the developer was considered an overgrown do-nothing, and some of the problems were overgrown ditches and weeds, while others were under-grown grass and trees.

But after the group got to thinking about how overgrown related to their problems, someone suggested that the owners take some of the weeds and plant them in their yards. Someone else suggested having a plant sale to raise money for a good lawyer while the next suggested having a plant sale and a neighborhood carnival to raise more money. Then another suggestion was made to invite the local media to take pictures and advertise the plight of the homeowners. Plans were made to have games and a pavilion with pictures and examples of the problems for the media. Someone else suggested that the developer be notified of the group's action. He was notified and at that point something was done about the problems. The carnival was held anyway and it raised over $3,000 for the group. The carnival became an annual affair and a swimming pool was built later. So overgrown started a chain of events that not only resolved

Make sure each contributor knows what the next person has to do. That knowledge will help them do their work more accurately so every part will fit together more easily. Also, establish progress checks. They help keep people honest in their use of time and allow for analysis if slippage or other problems occur.

6. Threat analysis

You are now ready for the most important, also most often neglected, part of the process. This part is the most important primarily because this is where you try to catch the mistakes, errors and inefficiencies that destroy a project. What are the things that can go wrong with your action plan? Making a blue sky list is one way to start. Include such items as peoples' ability or inability to carry through with their part, machine breakdowns, lack of timely support by your suppliers, delivery errors and slowdowns, weather changes, inflation, government interference or changes of policy. There literally are a million such possibilities. Are you going to worry about them all? No, but you need to concern yourself with those that are most likely to have an important negative impact on your plan.

The elements that will do the most damage should be your highest priority, even if they have a low probability of happening. Your car is a good example of a solution to your need for transportation. You may not believe you need an active threat analysis, as the car and loan companies, the government, have done them for you. You have a seat belt and air bag to help you in accidents. The government has a law that you must use the belt. Your loan company and the government insist you carry insurance. You have a spare tire and sometimes the gas gauge says you are empty even when you have more gas. The impact of not having insurance can be bankruptcy or fines or ruining other peoples' lives as well as your own. The impact of an accident is possible death, while the impact of a flat is added expense and a delay in your travel plans. Because the impact of a flat is less than the impact of the other problems, no state has passed a law that requires a spare tire.

Always have a plan B

There is also an issue with the probability of occurrence as well as the impact. Do you know that the probability of having an accident is at least three times more than the probability of having a flat tire? But consider that the impact of an accident is certainly much more than the impact of having a flat tire. So why do people not use their seat belts more often than they do? Time to buckle up and comfort are the two answers most often given. Imagine that; two very low priority reasons are given for not taking a precaution against the most significant issue for a driver: serious injury and death.

To determine the priorities about which contingencies you will consider first, look for those which could cause the most damage and which have the highest probability of occurring. Then consider those which could cause the most damage but are lower in probability of occurring. Then handle those that have a high probability of occurring but which will cause less damage. Consider this diagram:

	High Impact	Low Impact
High Probability	1st priority	3rd priority
Low Probability	2nd priority	4th priority

Many people like to deal with the easiest priorities, regardless of whether they have high impact or not. Before laws were passed, most people had spare tires but few buckled up. Ease of dealing with an issue has nothing to do with what the priorities should be. Often the high impact, high probability issues are the most difficult to deal with so they may only get cursory attention.

After you have determined the priority of your contingency plans, it is necessary to create an action plan to deal with them. There are three kinds of plans:

- preventive plans
- concurrent plans
- disaster plans.

A preventive plan, for example, could be changing the oil in a motor every 3,000 miles to prevent engine damage. Learn when the average negative event occurs and do what is necessary to eliminate the conditions that allow it to occur.

A concurrent plan is like a fire extinguisher. When the damage is occurring, throw in more customer service representatives, salespeople or double your advertising. The goal of a concurrent plan is to fight the damage so it is minimized.

The disaster plan is similar to fire insurance. After the damage has been done, what can be salvaged? Or how fast and effectively can you undo the damage. Every contingency, like fire, can have all three types of plans when you start early enough. If you do not plan preventions, then you have to fall back on concurrent plans, but if they are not planned or do not work, and if you do not get at the problem fast enough, the problem might become a disaster. So failure at this stage has the danger of being fatal to your entire problem solving effort. That is why FEMA's trailer program solution has been criticized so much: not numerous enough to service the problem and too late to make a positive difference.

7. Execute your plan

It is not enough to think about it, we do have to do it. Much has been written and discussed about the necessity of good execution in dealing with a problem. As the great coach Lombardi said: "Perfect practice makes perfect."

8. Evaluate results

How do you know you got it right, or any other result for that matter? You have to spend the time being honest with what your efforts have achieved. This stage is usually not difficult if you have done a good job of stating your objectives and made them measurable. Remember figures do not lie but reporters can; only meeting a due date is not sufficient information about the results you have achieved to allow a thorough evaluation. Once you do your evaluation you still have to determine if your goals have been reached or if there is more to be done. If your business problem is like most business problems, something still remains to be done: Increase your profit objectives. That is easy for any coach to figure out.

Some Final Reminders

Remember the eight steps. Memorize them and know where you are in the process so you do not get confused, repeat yourself or mislead the people whom you are coaching or who are trying to assist you. Help people stay on track when they are resolving their problems. Stay out of problems that are not yours. It is better to help others learn to resolve their own problems. That is what coaching is all about.

Be prepared for the times when you will be asked to participate in a situation where some of the steps have already been completed. Your boss may come in your office and say: Tom, do this for me please; or: Take a look at this and give me your opinion. In the first case, it appears the action has been planned, but most likely a threat analysis has not been. In the second case, has he shared his goals and priorities with you? In both cases, you will be able to perform better if you ask to have the other steps reviewed. Most importantly ask: What has already been done and how did they find and specify the problem? If you do not get that information, you may wander off into resolving a far different problem than the others have imagined. Get as much information about the problem solving efforts accomplished before the problem was passed to you.

Also many people believe that responding to an opportunity does not need a full problem–cause evaluation. Do not fall into that trap. If someone is offering you what they represent as a good deal and all you have to do is say yes to a good thing, remember to think through what is in it for them and what will be the actual costs to you to take advantage of their opportunity. You will want to do that before you say yes, especially if the opportunity does not materialize in the way they represented it. Ask yourself what problem(s) they are trying to resolve and how accepting their opportunity could create problems for you. A good coach helps his people know and assess the opportunities and threats when he passes on or delegates problems.

Questions to Ask Yourself
- Do I know why the problem solving steps are ordered the way they are?
- Do I understand the mistakes that can happen in each step?

- Could I be a good contributor to problem solving groups if I only keep track of where the group is in the process?
- What has to happen to teach others to observe the steps in the problem solving process?
- Can I really keep things straight when things get complicated?
- Can I tackle most any problem or am I limited to problems I studied in school or have seen before?
- Am I willing to jump into problems and learn how to resolve them better and more efficiently now that I know the steps in the process?
- Do I listen well enough to other people when they need my help?
- Am I too optimistic when I try to estimate the time necessary to plan and follow through on that plan?
- Do I know how to ask good questions when I ask others to help me solve a problem?
- Am I a good contributor to my group when we try to solve a problem?
- Am I anxious, afraid, or hesitant when I try to solve problems?
- If I am, how might I resolve those issues and become more confident as a problem solver?
- How can I best coach for good problem solving?

RESOURCES

Many beginning coaches have found reading and learning about creativity and problem solving very useful; here is an excellent book which will help you explore these important concepts.

Mindmapping: Your Personal Guide to Exploring Creativity and Problem Solving, Berkley Books, 1991.

8

Coaching Yourself

Does coaching yourself mean you should ask yourself a lot of questions? Yes. Every chapter in this book ends with a series of questions you could ask yourself. But coaching yourself means more than simply coming up with answers to those questions. It means being aware of how you use the answers to those questions to make changes in yourself. Experiencing how to make changes in yourself will assist you in helping others improve themselves.

The steps to improvement include:

> 1) Unconscious incompetence
>
> 2) Conscious incompetence
>
> 3) Conscious competence
>
> 4) Unconscious competence

Unconscious incompetence describes how one goes about one's daily existence, doing activities but being unaware of how one does them and what might be done to improve. To become aware you will have to watch yourself as you think and do. Conscious incompetence means you have made an effort to change yourself but you are not sure whether it has achieved the positive consequences you intend. As you try to improve, you may forget to implement the change you know you should or are not successful in your efforts. You have reached conscious competence when you persevere in trying to install the change again and again until you are regularly successful. You reach the stage of unconscious competence as you make your improvement a habit to the point that you do not have to think about it. Now you can spot another change you would like to make in your incompetence.

Can you see why watching yourself is an important step in being a coach? You have to know how to improve yourself before you can help others improve. Explaining the four steps of improvement to everyone you coach will help them improve their ability to make changes in themselves. Some may have already learned the four steps unconsciously. But knowing how to improve themselves consciously will help them learn to be coaches too. That is one quality of coaching that has not been mentioned yet: Coaches tend to multiply themselves because they pass on their insights so others can use them.

COACHING FOCUSES ON CHANGE EVERYDAY

The performance review was invented to change behavior. The manager and employee may have discussed changes on a more frequent basis but the consequences of how the employee has responded are usually not revealed until the performance review at the end of a year. How can that type of communication positively influence how changes are implemented? The flow of daily activity is the usual way of getting work done. The flow of daily activity should be the context of working on and evaluating changes.

Coaching has no holidays

As a coach you should look at performance on a daily basis. Examine yourself as you manage to question if there is anything you do which can be improved. Self awareness is the beginning of knowledge about things that need to be changed. Your self awareness will help you begin the change process as it is what you learn about yourself that will improve your ability to understand how to help others. Begin having a daily conversation with yourself about what you want to change in yourself. Keep track of which conversations work and which do not. Those conversations will inform you about what kinds of conversations might work with your employees.

SELF-RESPONSIBILITY CREATES COOPERATION

Passing the buck has been a standard way of responding ever since criticism was invented as a means of trying to create job change. What happened the last time you refused to accept responsibility to own up to a mistake and change yourself? Did the person you passed the buck to make any effort to change or did he just pass it on too? How did you feel about each other, trusting and cooperative, or angry and resentful? How much teamwork got accomplished the next time you tackled a tough assignment together? Likely more denial of responsibility unless one of your team stood up and dug into the task and pulled the rest of your group into it. Were you that leader? If you were, you know what damage passing the buck can cause but you also know what assuming responsibility feels like and what kind of effects they both have on others. It takes self-confidence to assume self-responsibility. It takes confidence and responsibility to be a coach. A coach with the experience of making changes in himself knows what self-responsibility feels like.

There is another aspect of self-responsibility that is important in coaching. Coaching seeks to develop cooperation in communications and problem solving. Cooperation in communication and problem solving build a common understanding of what it takes to work together while negotiating and resolving issues especially if a mistake has been made. Rallying together to clean up a common mistake often makes a team out of a group.

Teams work better together when each member is aware of what the other members can contribute. They ask clarifying questions of each other, they feel free to verbalize observations of what is happening in the team and the pace of progress it is making toward their objectives. They can bring a member up to speed more quickly about what happened when the member was absent. They know the questions that need to be asked to explore the cause of problems and how to work out complex action plans. They know that an action plan is not complete if a plan B has not been worked out.

It takes go-getters to make a team

If the team is still trying to figure out what the actual cause of the mistake was, but someone decides to present a solution, the group can point out that a solution is not appropriate at that particular time. Keeping everyone contributing the appropriate idea at the right time is a very important part of keeping the team on track. Individuals will always be thinking of different parts of the process because different ideas trigger different responses. But the individual needs to censure herself to contribute what the team needs at the time the team needs it, rather than blurt out her thoughts and steer the group off on a needless tangent. If you have been a part of a team that communicated and cooperated well together, you have a good basis for your coaching. You know what it takes to keep the group cooperating, on-track and reaching their goals more quickly.

When you have learned to follow good communications practices and the steps in good problem solving, you can model them for your group. A possible conversation:

E1: Why were we behind in our productivity goals last week?

E2: I think we ought to get another machine.

C: Do we really understand what the problem is yet?

E2: I know we just need another machine. I have been thinking about it all week.

C: That might be one answer. Do we really have a handle on what our basic problem is yet?

E3: Of course, I think all our machines are too slow.

C: Any other ideas?

E1: We were short on bottles. We probably need to make sure our supplier is holding up to his contract.

C: So there may be several causes. Other ideas?

E4: The power was out for a while. That might have had an effect. We need to make sure that does not happen again.

C: Good point, but before we start looking for what effects there might have been, do you think there are any other possible causes that should to be looked at?

E2: I do not think the power had much to do with it; it was only out at shift change.

C: Before we analyze the impact of any possible causes, why not make sure we have all the causes we think might be involved on the table because we will want to look at the one that could have had the most impact first to see if it had anything to do with the other things that might have gone wrong.

E5: I am new. There were several times when I had to stop the line to get some answers. Do you think that had any effect?

C: Could be. Can we think of anything else?

E5: Silence

C: OK. What have we got so far?

Notice that almost everyone has an idea of what might be wrong and a solution to his favorite problem. To allow the group to run off resolving just any of the suggested solutions could get the group mired in dealing with insignificant issues. The coach needs to be prepared to keep everyone on track. Keeping the group on track will not only help solve the most important problems but will help the group develop the discipline of dealing with first things first. As you help the group maintain its discipline, the group members themselves will learn to stay on track. They will also learn to make the statements that will help the group itself stay on track. When the group can discipline itself to stay on track, you will have to coach less and the whole process of analysis and action will happen more efficiently.

Your example of asking questions, staying on track and sorting out good answers will model the kinds of behaviors you want your employees to learn. Occasionally, you can point out some of the things you want them to learn. Pointing out learning objectives will help keep the task of learning in everyone's awareness and begin the process of making changes. Experiencing the success of learning will help people make it a habit. If you can keep yourself on track in the problem solving process how well do you think you could do as a coach trying to keep others on track?

There has been considerable research on change and learning in the business world. Much of it points to the fact that ideas examined and learned outside the workplace rarely get implemented in the workplace. It is hard to take a new idea and apply it to a job unless everyone on the team agrees with the new idea and is motivated to make the change. Left on their own, most people will merely do what they are accustomed to do. New ideas for change often get ignored and that ignorance can be the kiss of death to improvements. As a coach you will have to ask the same questions over and over again, call attention to the same things many times, and encourage learning and change consistently. It may take making the same mistake repeatedly to provide the motivation to make a change a habit. You will have to learn how to make change a habit before your group will develop the consistent focus on change that you will want them to develop. You will need to be the example of change before your employees will know what it takes for change to happen.

To become an effective coach, you must change from a person who wants others to change to a person who makes changes in herself then works with others to cement change in place. You must demonstrate to yourself, your boss, and your employees that you are motivated to be an example and that you know how to make that example be important to others. You must ask for, and receive, their understanding and support of your intention to change before you will have the credibility to ask them to change and to struggle with them through those changes.

Fortunately a coach does not have to know everything about every topic that might come up in your conversations about change. For some reason, though, if you call yourself a coach, employees sometimes have higher expectations of you than if they still see you as the average manager. The common view of coaches is they have superhuman capabilities. You may aspire to developing that level of capability but initially and for some time you will be testing your wings as a coach.

You may have an excellent technical background and that background likely got you to your present position. But as an aspiring coach you need to test yourself in as many situations as possible, not by telling people all the things you know but by comparing what you know with what your direct reports know. The primary way of comparing yourself is by listening to what they say, observing what they do and helping them process the difficulties in making their changes while you share the difficulties you have faced in making improvements.

Asking people to explain what they do and why they do it is a reasonable way to start. Everyone will be curious about the purpose of your questions. Learning is your best answer; have you found that posing good questions to yourself stimulates thinking and learning? Actually, listening begins the process of formulating a question before you actually ask it. Then asking a question focuses your attention on the answer you expect to hear not because you want to hear that answer but because predicting an answer requires you to examine what you know about a situation. When an answer comes that you have not predicted, you have an opportunity to ask yourself why your prediction did not materialize. The more your predictions materialize, the better you understand your people and their situations and the more capable you will be in helping them resolve those situations. But be careful when you predict an answer to your question that you fail to listen properly and that you do not end up always giving out your predicted answer after your employee has shared their answer. You need to work with their answer rather than your own. Your own answer is useful only as a check on your own thinking.

Another key to coaching yourself is to feel comfortable in your helping skills. People will ask you questions you will not know the answer to. Be honest. Never say you know something when you do not. Giving bad advice is worse than admitting ignorance. Determine who should look for the answer. Do not always make it the other person. You can do some research too. After you indicate what you have found out, ask if they understand it. Also ask them to explain how they see your answer working in their situation. Help is not just finding possible answers. Help means applying possible answers and using your combined wisdom to see if the possible answer works.

So, are you ready to make some changes in your management style? Which ones do you feel like making? What new skill do you think would be valuable for you to add to the way you manage? Perhaps the discussion has given you some ideas that will help you understand why problems in communication and problem solving come up and how to improve them. On the other hand, learning how to ask non-threatening questions might be a good place to start.

Questions to Ask Yourself

- Have you compared your skills to the job you have to perform as a manager?
- How do you rate yourself?
- Where do you need to do better?
- What changes do you need to make?
- What will it take for you to make those changes?
- Do you think you have the ability to make the changes you need to make?
- What kind of risks will you be taking as you make those changes?
- What could go wrong and what should you be prepared to do if you are not capable of making those changes?
- How many times have you stopped the buck at your desk?
- Can you be objective with yourself?
- Do you understand the relationship between self-honesty and cooperation with others?
- Where would you like to start your efforts to coach?

RESOURCES

As you advance in your coaching and mentoring skills, here is an excellent book which will build your confidence and knowledge:

Coaching, Counseling & Mentoring, Amacom, 1999.

9

Coaching Your Boss

The title of this chapter may be a little misleading. Becoming a coach does not imply you have the authority or responsibility to act as a coach to your boss. You may still ask him questions though. And you know your boss will have something to say about whether or not you can assume the role of coach to your direct reports and how far he will let you take your coaching. He has an interest in keeping matters in his department orderly and predictably within his control. He may see your addition of coaching to your management style as upsetting the apple cart if he is afraid of any of the changes that your new management style might make in his department. Does it not make sense for you to get him on your side before you practice your coaching skills? It is your ability to get him on your side that will determine your future as a coach. This chapter will explore how you might approach him.

Bosses Are Never the Same

Your boss is likely a multi-faceted person. But the relevant characteristics which describe your boss for the purposes of your developing into a coach include basically two dimensions: 1) Does your boss use questions well or does he need to develop better skills in how to use questions to facilitate job learning? 2) Does your boss take the task of helping his employees learn on their jobs seriously or does he busy himself with directing and controlling them while turning the learning task over to someone else? These two dimensions can be organized into a matrix describing four different types of bosses relative to the important dimensions of questioning and learning:

	Turns employees learning over to others	Takes employee learning seriously as a part of his job
Tends to micromanage; needs to adopt the use of questions for learning	Type A boss	Type B boss
Uses questions to facilitate learning	Type C boss	Type D boss

The Type A boss is a qualitatively different person from the other bosses. He may use questions but his questions are employed mainly to elicit simple information from his direct reports rather than to foster their thinking. His questions usually take the form of: When did you do this? Why did you not think of that? You learned that in your last job, did you not? Do you have the figures for the last month ready? To whom are you going to give your results from job X? And so forth. In addition to eliciting information he may use questions to impress people with his knowledge or to emphasize his disappointment in their capabilities: Did I not tell you how to do that better the last time we talked? Did you learn that in my department, how could you?

In addition, the Type A boss shows little interest in working with his direct reports to facilitate their learning. What little interest he shows may come from a recognition that people could improve job skills, but his focus is usually on their present job achievement rather than on the future skills that the company may need to develop in their employees. Also, he may focus on other ways of assisting your co-workers to learn. He may prefer to have your company pay for college classes if you have an education benefit. He may prefer to send people to your company courses or bring in outside trainers. In any of those cases he likely sees the priorities of his job as different than a coach might see them. Instead of focusing on the collaborative functions of learning and problem solving, he likely prefers to employ the more centralizing functions of planning, organizing, directing and controlling.

If you have this type of boss, your desire to add coaching skills to your management style may be a considerable stretch for him. As he does not practice assisting your co-workers to learn through questions; he may insist that you manage your direct reports in the same way he does. Even if he does not insist on it, it is likely that he will show a reluctance to accept your coaching goals because of his unfamiliarity with how you will be able to achieve your overall management objectives.

Where does your boss need help?

In either case, he will benefit from an introduction to the goals and processes of coaching in order to acquaint him about the direction in which you want to grow your management skills. As he is familiar with training courses, one introduction may be to ask him to consider attending a course on coaching at the university or through a private vender. Another introduction might be to ask him to read this book. A third introduction might be to engage a coaching professional to discuss how coaching could be added to his as well as your coaching style. In any case, be prepared to explore as many avenues as possible to help your boss understand how important others have found learning on the job to be. Help him see that improving the people within the company to handle future operations is an opportunity to grow with the company.

He could respond negatively to your suggestions that he change even if you explain how his growth would benefit your co-workers. He depends upon your support in helping him maintain his tried and true methods. As any change you suggest might be seen as betrayal on your part, avoid exposing yourself to his resentment. Help him consider how others have suggested how improvements might be made through employee learning. Find articles or quotes from authorities that will help him consider learning as an important business enterprise. And help him understand how he can personally benefit when improvements are installed on his watch.

The Type B boss takes on-the-job learning seriously but has not yet discovered the role questioning can play in facilitating that learning. You can be more direct with this type of boss than the bosses who do not understand how on-the-job learning works. She understands that job experience creates skills.

Though she does not understand how questions foster thinking, she knows that learning can be facilitated. You should be able to talk with her about how you ask yourself probing questions and how they would work with your direct reports. You can relate how using questions to explore ideas has helped you in your own search for ideas about change. You can wonder out loud if she sees how such questions can open up paths to change and if she thinks her department could use and support an increase in the number of change ideas that might come out of your coaching efforts. You should get her support for putting more changes into effect as she should understand that change is the direct result of on-the-job learning. Help her see that learning without putting that learning into effect can result in frustration and disappointment for the employee.

The Type C boss understands that learning can be fostered through questions but prefers to turn over the learning function of his management to others. While he knows that a well-placed question can focus an employee on researching a problem, he probably prefers to send some of your co-workers to training courses both internally and outside the company. Consequently, he may not routinely engage in walking through problem solving efforts to the same extent that a coach might. He may use questions primarily to stimulate your co-workers to get into immediate issues that need their attention, while ignoring areas of management learning that would be useful to your colleagues for their long-term advancement. His style may also limit his understanding of how learning encourages making improvements on the job. His focus is primarily on getting the job done right now.

The Type C boss understands that his management functions include more than his doing the work of planning, controlling, etc. He sees that learning for the future is important but he is shortsighted when it comes to understanding that learning is more effective on the job and that his management style needs to include a stronger emphasis on assisting his direct reports to develop. Rather than suggest yourself that he develop that skill, find an article or two that addresses how people learn on-the-job and give them to him. Ask if he read them and what his thoughts are about their content. If his mind is open to improving his own attention to on-the-job learning, you could then introduce your own interest in developing a coaching style. Get his support and assure him you will share your learning with him. He might then be open to looking at this book, for instance.

If your manager remains closed to the idea of on-the-job learning and developing a questioning coaching style, you may need to enlist the help of your human resource department or a colleague at his level who are open to coaching and on-the-job learning. They could add their insights and support to those that your articles provide, and so assist your boss to accept your efforts.

The Type D boss is usually an excellent type of boss to have. He fits well into the relevant descriptions of this book. He takes learning seriously and seeks to impart learning in a supportive way. He encourages thought and change on-the-job. He may have given you this book as a means of fostering your growth and advancement. But if he did not, he should understand your desire to move into a more active role in working with your direct reports to assist their learning and becoming a change agent in their job roles. He likely rewards those who report to him for their efforts to gain new knowledge and to use that knowledge in improving communications and problem solving processes that are important to your business success. When you talk to him about your desire to become a more questioning person and to use that means of stimulating thought in your direct reports as a coach, he should understand and encourage your efforts. You may wish to observe him as he talks with your co-workers in an effort to see how he uses questions and encourages his direct reports to learn and change. He may have already incorporated some coaching skills in how he manages without labeling them as coaching. If he does not have a copy of this book, you may consider referring him to it. It should be relatively easy to get his support for your coaching efforts, and he may share his ideas about managing for your learning.

You may be lucky. You may be reading this book because your boss is a coaching manager who has challenged you to add coaching to your management capabilities. If this is the case, he likely has tried to establish a working atmosphere where learning and skill improvement are a regular part of your responsibilities. He should be a good resource for you as you try to develop the coaching skills you seek. Take advantage of her or him as the case may be! Watch how she works with you and check out alternative ways of approaching communications and problem solving issues so you can expand your understanding and capacity to deal with conflict and job-skill difference issues. Ask her if you might take on some team leading situations while she observes how you work through action plans to achieve goals, then discuss the various different possible ways of how questions help employees focus on developing job skills. You will learn coaching more adequately through experience than through reading.

It is entirely possible that your boss may not be described adequately by any of these types. Thinking people warn that individuals should not be pigeon-holed and typecast as such efforts limit the ability to understand a person in their reality. Your boss is certainly more than any of these types discussed. The types mentioned here only look at two dimensions of management when there are actually dozens. The types suggested here are only described in an effort to help you look at your boss from the points of view of two of the primary emphases of being a coach. There may be many reasons why your boss would support or deny your interests in adding coaching skills to your management efforts. Unfortunately, it is not within the scope of this book to discuss all the possible ways in which a boss could react to your interests. You will have to deal with the specific issues your boss presents to you whether or not they can be found in this book.

Still, the question of how to use typing for understanding is a basic issue in the field of coaching. Each work situation has individual elements that do not fit into any group of types. And each work situation has, at the same time, elements that can be classified into types such as problems of communication, problem solving, physics, chemistry, human relations, teamwork, etc. As a coach, it is your responsibility to help your employees to sort out the common elements of type and associate the individual issues that color each specific situation. Much learning can be achieved in associating facts specific to an individual situation with the types of information and knowledge that guide your thinking. But it is the presence of the individual non-typical elements of each situation that present the employee and yourself with the opportunity to be creative and so allow you to add your insight as to how changes can be made which could contribute to your skills as a coach and the progress of your company.

BOSS SAYS NO TO YOUR COACHING

How might you respond if your boss gives you a flat no to your desire to add coaching to your management style? A few bosses have not wanted their managers to add coaching, mostly because they believe that there is little need for the employees in their department to learn to improve on the job. Those bosses believe that everyone in their department is functioning at their peak performance level and if they do not function at the expected level, they should be terminated. As a manager for that type of boss, your task is likely one of making sure every employee functions at their benchmark speed and efficiency most if not all of the time, including yourself.

If you work in that type of atmosphere, you know the pressure that the job puts on people. It is impossible that every employee feels entirely comfortable with that type of job and that level of pressure. In fact, if you are working in that type of situation, you have most likely felt the pressure on many an occasion and it may be that pressure that has led you to explore the possibility of relieving the pressure, at least for yourself, through coaching. Please do not buy into the idea that coaching is not applicable to that kind of work situation. After all, screaming coaches who pile on the pressure still get work out, customers satisfied, and profits made. It is also true that coaches who do not scream while still pushing people to produce results can be successful. Screaming is not the only thing that can be omitted in a high pressure situation.

As a manager in a high pressure situation, your emphasis may shift somewhat from assisting your employees change the job to helping your employees change themselves. Remember, coaching focuses on the individual rather than the job. Your discussions and questions will be primarily related to the ability of each individual to improve their own efficiency and effectiveness rather on job improvement. Help your employees become more comfortable in their jobs through understanding how they perform the physical and mental tasks that keep them flawlessly sharp and up-to-speed. Instead of using work time to discuss problems, use their break or lunch time to become acquainted and build interpersonal trust. Find out what they do to deal with the pressure and build their efficiency.

After you ask an individual if they will allow you to share their secrets, pass them on to others, perhaps with a newsletter which includes your own insights. For those who have difficulty with the pressure, you can ask them the questions that will help them make the decision about leaving. You do not have to call yourself a coach, even though your focus is assisting your employees to improve their performance or leave which in turn should benefit your team and your business. All that glitters is not gold. Those who help all succeed need not be called coaches either. You and your boss can choose what you are called.

Questions to Ask Yourself

- How will your boss respond to your desire to be a coach?
- Are you prepared to discuss with him the benefits and handle his objections?
- Does your boss exhibit any management or coaching skills that you can emulate?
- Will your company in general welcome your efforts to coach?
- Does the culture of your company support on-the-job learning?
- How might you adapt the practice of coaching to your company's management style?

RESOURCES

Managing up, or in this case, coaching up, is never easy. An excellent resource is:

> *Coaching at the Executive Level (How to Coach the Coach),* Center for Coaching and Mentoring; visit *www.coachingandmentoring.com/articles.*

10
How Well Do You Stack Up?

So far you have had a tour of what it takes to be a coach: what coaches do, what they do not do, the risks of being a coach and what it will take to obtain the support of your boss and your employees. What do you think so far? Are you ready to start adding coaching to your management style? Many managers have. They are finding the process of becoming a coach challenging but rewarding. They are finding it takes more than wanting to be a coach to be a coach. They are finding it takes thought and a willingness to experiment to build the foundation for how they interact with their co-workers and direct reports. They are finding building a relationship of trust to be a necessary part of how they go about becoming a coach. They are finding there are many personal qualities and skills that go into becoming a coach.

THE COACHING DIMENSION

This chapter will help you explore additional aspects of how a coach works and the behaviors that support those skills. This chapter will present many dimensions of interpersonal competencies and organizational capabilities that contribute to effective coaching. Please understand that it is not a requirement to be a coach that you possess each and every competency and capability to the Nth degree. After all, you are just starting to become aware of coaching and what it will take to pursue your coaching endeavors. Coaching is a learning process for everyone including the coach. Some managers may wonder if they have the necessary skills for the responsibilities of coaching.

Coaches never stop learning

One basic necessity is to know how to be a supportive person but it is also necessary to know how to confront people upon whom you depend even though you may have a fear of offending them. Failure to resolve this inner conflict may render it very difficult for you to function as a coach effectively.

Still, you have already been given the authority to be a manager. You already have the responsibility to interact with your employees to help them focus and improve their work efforts. You already have the responsibility to offend people if it will take offense to move them to embrace their responsibilities to achieve their work goals. But adopting coaching as a management skill will help you mitigate the necessity of offending people. The more your employees see you as a helper the less they will be prone to see you as someone with whom they should take offense.

As you lead them to build skills, especially those skills that have been challenging or even dumbfounding them, the more you will be seen as a resource whom they can consult and depend upon even if you ask challenging questions and do not give ready made answers. Remember, it is on the foundation of a helping relationship that coaching works. Coaching seeks to eliminate the fight between the worker and management. Coaching seeks to eliminate the bad-guy, good-guy standoff. Coaching seeks to make everyone good-guys when everyone wins because everyone builds a better future through better skills and more productivity. Coaching seeks to face and overcome those challenges that people hate and fear. However, you and your employees need not fear making a mistake because you will have helped your employees learn through their mistakes. You are just another regular person who learns when things go awry. You are not a flawed and despised manager who forces employees into the meat grinder of drudgery and fatigue. Congratulations, you are a human being like everyone else.

Are you ready to look at more attributes that may contribute to good coaching? Rate yourself please, by putting a number from seven (the left side describes me) to one (the right side describes me) between each paring.

I am a good listener	7 6 5 4 3 2 1	Poor listener
Want others to succeed first		I want to succeed first
Tend to be honest		May be dishonest on occasion
Tend to be patient		Tend to be impatient
Make judgments carefully		Tend to make snap judgments
My questions are clear		My questions need more clarity
I am confident I think logically		I need to be more logical
Know how to deal with time pressure		Time sometimes gets away from me
Deliver on what I promise		I have been known to disappoint others
Know how to put things positively		I tend to see many things negatively
Can ask for help when I need it		I have trouble asking for help
Learning is important to me		Learning can be too much work
Like to be challenged		I have been known to run from challenge
Learn any way I can		I give up when learning gets confusing
Analyze things well		I need help when I analyze something
Know consequences of what I do		I do not worry about the effects of my behavior

	7 6 5 4 3 2 1	
Look for new ways to solve problems		Usually do what I know best
Can work through ambiguity		Need clarity all the time
Can wait for answers		Need answers now
Can work for change		Prefer to keep things the same
Can juggle more than one change		Juggling changes is beyond me
Am receptive to new ideas		Have trouble with new ideas
Welcome complex problems		Have difficulty with complexity
Work to overcome obstacles		Obstacles stop me on occasion
Tend to be bold		Tend to be hesitant
Will take a calculated risk		Risk is exciting
Prefer to be pragmatic		Just like to do things
Know myself well		Do not spend time thinking about who I am
Confident		Diffident
Assertive		Wait to be lead
Gregarious		Shy
Curious		Would rather be having fun
Trust myself		Like someone to be around if necessary
Trust others		Guarded
Persevere		Have been known to give up at times
Comfortable with details		Details bore me
Like to receive feedback		Do not bother me with your opinions

	7 6 5 4 3 2 1	
Like to give honest feedback		Do not like to disappoint anyone
Look others in the eye		That looking-in-the-eye stuff bothers me
Friendly		I like to be by myself
Like to know what is going on		I am curious only occasionally
Know that a team can do what I cannot		Being in a team is a lot of work
Know how to deal with stress		Run from stress
Cooperative		More competitive
Want to get ahead		I am fine where I am
Am comfortable being a boss		Being a boss is too much work
Work toward goals		Just tell me what to do
Like problems others bring me		I like my own problems
Like to negotiate		Just tell me what it costs and what I get
Like to increase productivity		I have a speed at which I am most comfortable

There are 50 pairs. A score of 200 puts you barely on the left side which describes those who take up coaching and tend to do well. But these descriptions are only a place to start. No pair will magically make a coach out of you by itself. If you consistently gave yourself a higher score for items on the left you may not have been as honest with yourself as you might have. Everyone has some lower scores. Low scores mean you could be a better coach by improving yourself in this area. Learning to improve yourself is good experience to help you understand the tasks of coaching.

You may not know how to rate yourself on some attributes. Who in your organization can you speak to? Can your boss help you? Will you need a coach to understand yourself better? If you had a coach what would you want to work on?

A Starting Point

Start where you are. Establish your goals. Write down the kinds of capabilities you want to develop as you improve as a coach. Writing down goals helps in this process. Choose the most important three goals and write down what you will do to achieve them. When you improve sufficiently on one goal establish another one. Keep three goals in front of you if you can.

Good coaches learn how to think like their employees, otherwise they remain strangers

---

Please do not be disappointed and put off by not reaching a goal. Some coaches always make easy goals to achieve. Other coaches have at least one goal that will be difficult and will take some effort to achieve, such as finishing a degree. Others realize a goal is too tough for now and choose something that is important to achieve right now. Learn to take different approaches for establishing and working on your goals. That way you learn the different ways your employees might approach working on their goals. Follow with an analysis of each of your direct reports: what kind of people are they? How will a specific effort on your part meet with success or failure with that particular person? Examine why you think so. What does each person need to do in order to qualify for your job? How can you best coach them? Write down what you will do to establish and maintain communication with them. What kinds of discussions do you expect from each? How much positive effort do you expect from each? Think about their response to problems when you meet with them individually. Will they be a different person with you in meetings? When you have answered these questions for each of your direct reports and done an analysis of their jobs and how they fit (as discussed in chapter one) you should be ready to ask some good questions. You will be on your way as a coach.

Questions to Ask Yourself

- Do I have a good idea of the qualities that I can build on to become a coach?
- Have I been successful in creating beneficial change in previous jobs?
- Have I made changes in my personal life that have helped me achieve goals?
- Have I been able to make changes in my relationships with people that have benefitted both of us?
- Have I looked at some of the ways I do things and found improvements I can make?
- Do I understand how changes are approved in my company?
- Have I seen how changes in processes have influenced the direction of my company?
- Do I believe the management of my company encourages their employees to make changes?
- Do I know how to help my employees have their ideas fairly evaluated by the management of my company?
- Can I estimate how hard one of my employees will work to have an idea adopted by our company?
- How do I help managers above me assess how much impact a change will have on their operations?
- Are people who try to make changes rewarded or ignored in my company?
- Does the management in my company evaluate change suggestions fairly?
- Does the management in my company prefer the status quo over making a change?
- Have I found the 10 personal characteristics that will help me coach?
- Have I found the 10 personal characteristics that I need to improve to be a good coach?
- Have I found any characteristics that I must change to create cooperative relationships?

- Can I be surprised by something new to the point I might not be able to consider it objectively?
- Might I meet an idea or a person that I would respond to with fear as a coach?
- Can I be truly honest with someone with whom I have a disagreement?
- Can I help an employee find resources in our company that might be hard to find?

RESOURCES

Listening and conflict resolution are some of the most important parts of coaching; to learn more about these topics, consider reading:

People Skills; How to Assert Yourself, Listen to Others, and Resolve Conflicts, Simon & Schuster, 1997.

11

Perfect Practice Makes Perfect

You have confirmed to yourself that you have many of the necessary skills and perspectives to make coaching a part of your management style. Your boss is encouraging. Your employees appear to have welcomed the opportunity to look at their jobs and how they do them with your help. Now where do you start your coaching activities?

CAN CHANGE HAPPEN?

You start with the knowledge that research in businesses and other organizations shows that between half and two-thirds of organizational change efforts fail. It appears that managers and employees are capable of designing change programs that are more challenging than their ability to implement them. So be alerted to the fact that it takes more to make a change than just wanting to make it.

There has been a widely held belief in businesses and with many coaches that changes should be blessed at the top and then should filter down into the organization. Unfortunately, this belief has not been demonstrated by wide spread success. On the other hand most successful change has been shown to begin on a small scale. That means change happens as the result of personal growth, learning and unlearning, then matched with the support of other individuals who are interested in its success on a wider scale. Thus at the beginning there is no one person in charge of a project; rather there are individuals who compare ideas, try them out in discussions among themselves and determine what their positive benefits are.

Your role as a coach begins with an individual who looks at his job and wants to make a change. Before the change is implemented, you help the individual look at all the issues that the change entails: What mechanical or personnel process is involved, what resources are required to make the change and how far the change reaches into the organization? Reach means how many people and capital resources are affected. The further a change reaches, the more others need to be consulted about their responsibilities and their approval given. Please do not force your employees to select projects that promise to change the whole company. That may scare them away from working any change at all.

One change can reach everywhere

Help your employee predict how those in authority will respond. Many changes will require higher levels of authority than just those who are directly touched by the change. You may need to give your own approval and it may be necessary to get your boss' approval and his assistance in obtaining the approval of other managers at her level or higher.

Be careful not to underestimate the reach of a change. People do not like surprises. Help your employee understand that there may be differences in the perception of right and wrong by different managers in your company and that some of their perspectives may be perceived as irrational to your employee. It may take several conversations with different levels of management to gain the perspective necessary to evaluate a change and determine if it will be accepted or rejected by everyone affected by the reach of the change. But every conversation will help your employee gain perspective on how change is perceived and processed in your organization.

Help your employee see that changes, which have a small reach may have a better chance of getting implemented and those changes may be the best place for your employees to start. But avoid telling them you know that an idea with a long reach will not fly with someone. They must experience themselves the reluctance and struggle with the attempts to make the change acceptable to a particular person even if they are not successful. The experience of presenting and having his ideas considered will help your employee learn how others look at what he does so he can learn how to represent his next idea. Help your employee understand that having an idea rejected is not a failure but a learning process that will give his next idea a better chance of being accepted.

Your employee has to first past your acceptance test. Then he must pass the acceptance tests of everyone else who is touched by his idea. Passing these tests to acceptance is the perfect practice that makes change in your organization perfect. Without that practice, no idea for change will ever be adopted. Without that practice you will not learn how good a coach you are.

CHANGE TAKES TIME

Please do not assume that your coaching is not valuable if none of your employees' ideas get adopted right away. Each organization installs certain criteria for the acceptance of an idea. A company must do so otherwise a lot of worthless ideas will use up a lot of resources without any positive return. Help your employees understand that an organization must conserve resources so those ideas which are accepted will receive adequate resources necessary to make a true difference to your company. Help your employee understand that he used company resources to get his idea considered and that those resources were invested in his learning and growth. Your company gave him something valuable that he can take with him for the rest of his life. Your company gave him you as a coach and the gift of the best opinions his company has to offer. There will be a next time and he and you will be better prepared to move a change idea forward.

Your employees will ask you some questions to which your answer will likely be difficult for them to accept. Some people may judge you poorly if you must give them an unpopular or negative response. In this situation preface your remarks with: You may not like this answer. If you do not, please know that we can talk about it and try to work it through. Or: You may not like this answer and I am almost certain you will not like the fact that this answer is not negotiable. How do you think you will respond to this? My responsibility is to work with you no matter what direction you think you need to take.

Every journey begins with a single step according to the Chinese proverb. So does good coaching.

Yesterday, the employee you coached through the change implementation process came to you again with more thought on her original suggestion to make a change that would add significantly to your company's bottomline. She worked out the specifics of why the situation exists; what to do about it; (she presented an exhaustive analysis of all the possible alternatives and explained why the one she wants to implement should be the most efficient and effective one); who should do what and when; what approvals are required; specified the potential problems that might get in the way of completing the project successfully; and what should be done about them. She also calculated the exact amount the change would cost and its internal rate of return (better than your company's requirement for adoption). Finally, she cleared all the schedules of the people involved and got the commitment for their involvement from each of their departments. She did all this and you did not even assign her the project (but she did keep you posted as to her progress). She demonstrated she learned to ask herself all the questions you coached her to ask and to take initiative to get things rolling.

Congratulations, you have done a fantastic job of coaching her through the elements of the effort that goes into getting a change analyzed and off the ground. Your task now together is to confirm her analysis and the approval process, and get things started. After this one change demonstrates its value, then see what other projects she can handle and where in your organization she can fit to contribute her skills. If you coached her, why do you not do the same for all of your employees? Then apply for a well-deserved promotion. You can get promoted more easily when you have demonstrated you know how to coach effectively and there is someone capable of taking your place. Give yourself a pat on the back; you have accomplished the goal you set out to achieve.

> ## Questions to Ask Yourself
> - Are you ready to coach?
> - With whom will you start?
> - How will you start?
> - When will you start?
> - How far can you go?

RESOURCES

One more quality book for building and improving your coaching skills:

Real Time Coaching: How to Make the Minute by Minute Decisions That Unleash the Power in Your People, Leadership Horizons, 1999.

Additional copies of this book are available from the author. If you wish to discuss coaching, training, consulting, seminars. meetings, speeches or other program needs, or to examine additional publications by Dr. Fenger, he may be reached through his website: *www.tnfleadercoach.com*.